CHRISTISIS

HIGHER SOUL CULTURE

First Edition 1911
Reuben Swinburne Clymer

New Edition 2021
Edited by Tarl Warwick

CHRISTISIS

COPYRIGHT AND DISCLAIMER

The first edition of this work is in the public domain having been written prior to 1926. This edition, with its cover art and format, is all rights reserved.

In no way may this text be construed as encouraging or condoning any harmful or illegal act. In no way may this text be construed as able to diagnose, treat, cure, or prevent any disease, injury, symptom, or condition.

CHRISTISIS

FOREWORD

This slightly odd little text, written by Reuben Clymer, seeks to fuse the scientific and the spiritual under the banner of "Christisis"- a sort of metaphoric label for divine truth, and for initiatory practice. Much of the premise here is to engage in mindfulness and thereby to banish evil or lower thoughts in favor of ascending spiritually, for various purposes. This "Christisis" is given a sort of corporeal meaning and is labeled a "coming savior"- a fusion of spiritual and of social reform, to improve mankind in sundry ways.

While this book stresses belief in the specifically Judeochristian god, it also introduces essentially Hindu or Buddhist style breathing exercises and the use of meditation in order to reorient the mind towards positive and noble goals, and it admonishes the reader to partake in positive, healthy living techniques which are more from the spiritualist, or at least new age, movements, as opposed to those of the more Orthodox Christian path. It even mentions mantras (mantrams) as opposed to prayer, *per se*.

This edition of "Christisis" has been carefully edited for format and content. Care has been taken to retain all original intent and meaning.

CHRISTISIS

FOREWORD

In placing these instructions of "Success and Soul Culture" before the student, I do not think it necessary to give any prolonged explanation because they explain themselves as you progress in the work.

However, a word of explanation may be of value to the earnest student, especially since religion is so often mentioned. The student may say that he has a religion and does not need any other. I grant this, but does he really know what religion means?

On the other hand, these lessons may be taught to many of the millions, who, belonging to some church, are still seeking for something beyond. They are satisfied with the church, but there is something within them that is seeking continually for something, they know not what.

Thus we have two kinds of students, the one seeking success upon the material plane, the other seeking something which he possibly calls scientific interpretation of religion. In these instructions the sincere student will find both, for as he travels the path and develops or illuminates both mind and soul, he will find that in the Christisis are success, science and religion.

You, my student, believe that there is a God, or, if you will, an infinite something which is, which rules and in whom all things exist.

You must admit this or you must deny life. Accepting this fact you must admit that this Infinite Being, this Infinite Something, or God, is in all fixings and works through all things.

CHRISTISIS

If you accept this much, what difference will it make whether you are priest or politician, whether a farmer or a shepherd? God being the life principle in everything, ruling everything, He must as necessarily be in you, a politician, as He would be were you a minister of the Gospel.

It being impossible to contradict this, you must also recognize the fact that no matter what your vocation may be, if you are really a success, which means that if you are really working in harmony with divine law, your work, though it is politics, is to you a religion. If it is not, then your work is being accomplished under wrong conditions; you are working in and for darkness or the evil one.

Therefore, in this great work of self-development, no matter what your vocation may be, you will think of that development and its expression in your vocation as your religion. Experience soon teaches that this work demands a systematic understanding of truth, and a systematic training, and as such it becomes a science. Thus we have the wedding of science and religion, or, as we choose to call it, the Christisis.

Furthermore, understanding this great law, the student will no longer have one day out of seven set aside for worship and for religion. He will worship and have a religion for every day in the week and every hour of the day, because his vocation, no matter what it is, is his religion since he works under the Divine Law.

Therefore, the coming mankind will be a truly religious mankind, because science will be religion and religion will be science. This can only be accomplished by uniting the two, by bringing forth the Christisis. This is the spiritual life of the East and the material life of the West brought together into one harmonious expression. It is the giving of equal consideration to woman as to man, regarding her his equal, for all these things are in Christisis. R. Swinburne Clymer.

CHRISTISIS

LESSON ONE

As the student comprehends truth and realizes that he can daily develop within himself, now, the true likeness and image of Christisis, his struggles will become less painful, because he begins to recognize what he really wishes to accomplish and has faith that he can accomplish it.

With the new conditions come new powers; the student becomes conscious of his ability to use all his faculties. He begins to realize that he can regenerate his will and work in the spirit. The basis of his work will be spiritual and the being which he creates within himself and which gives him all powers is a spiritual or soul being; it is that which we call the Christisis.

Gradually he learns to know what the mind is. He begins to realize why he has a mind and he begins to recognize the power of that mind when rightly used.

In due time the student realizes that the mind is a dynamo and that it generates power and even has creative force. He learns to know that he is the mechanic who has the dynamo in charge and that the dynamo can create only the power (thought) which he allows it to create.

He then begins to center his mind upon the building of a wonderful temple, a temple not made with hands nor with sound of hammer. This temple is the soul. He builds it day by day, thought by thought, until he becomes the Christisis.

As he thus develops he will have clearer insight into all things. Nothing will trouble him for a long time; all things will be as one to him, for he has laid prejudice aside and he knows that all things that are are for some use and are required in the building of his temple, just as the rough wood is necessary in the building of a

CHRISTISIS

house. Man was placed upon earth to be a builder and this is the meaning of that beautiful allegory concerning the Temple of Sol-om-on. Man also must build such a temple as did Sol-om-on. This temple is the soul. It is that which will be known in the coming religion as the Christisis.

Man must be a creator. God has placed him upon earth so that he might create. What then must he create? He must create harmony, for to do this is to develop divinity.

He must overcome, for unless he overcomes he is weak and will always remain weak. Only the soul that overcometh is might. You ask what he is to overcome? His selfishness. Selfishness stands in the way of all true development; man's selfishness must be changed, transmuted into love and the feeling of brotherhood.

Remember that the soul is what we make it. We make or create it by the thoughts that we think. Thought-mastery is the fundamental basis of all true building and unless our thoughts are pure we cannot build a beautiful and perfect temple.

What, then, is the Creator? The thoughts we hold are the creator of our character. We can hold or entertain any thought that we wish. It depends upon us whether such thoughts shall be constructive or destructive.

In the religion of old it was said that "He that saith I know Him and keep not his commandments, is a liar and the Truth (God) is not in him." If we have the Divine nature developed to any extent at all we do know Him, we also know where He is, and what He is, and where He dwells or lives.

True religion is no longer considered as something which is good only on Sundays. It is becoming a living, vital thing. It is becoming something which we must follow and obey if we wish

CHRISTISIS

to be successful in any walk of life. Religion is coming to be considered as that which we are, that which we build now and for all time to come. True religion is a law, a law of life which no one can disobey with- out paying the penalty.

As the student builds this temple, this wonderful soul, he will learn to live not only in harmony with his own soul, but in harmony with all souls; his discriminating faculty will become keen, clear, penetrating, yet always tempered with the warm atmosphere of his loving heart. The true life can only he based on strict justice, he will be a brother to all, and this exact justice must always be allied with that supreme quality which embraces all things- Love.

The Masters of old have told us that the "Word became flesh and dwelt among us."

This is not an idle saying, but an exact statement of truth, and every student can verify it. The Word is simply that which is truth. It is that which teaches man the truth, that which teaches him the almighty power, that which teaches him to build a powerful mind and a soul that nothing on earth can overcome.

To make the Word flesh is nothing more nor less than to build these truths into the soul. It is the material wherewith we must build the Temple of the Christisis, which the ancient Masters called the Living God. Every student can make the Word flesh that it may dwell with him. He need but think the thoughts of truth, and live accordingly; thus gradually he erects that temple which is mighty, not only in a religious sense, but in a material sense as well, fur such an one will be successful in his chosen work since a powerful mind can control all things.

In the continued practice of correct thinking and right, living there will come to the student an increasing readiness to adjust the thoughts, words and actions from the spiritual point of

CHRISTISIS

view. With this practice will come an increase of knowledge, the knowledge of how definitely to adjust one's self to every relation in the natural and material life. The knowledge of how to obtain the influx of life, light and power from above will also come with this; therefore the student gains a threefold benefit. He gains spiritual life and power; he learns how to adjust this power so as to use it in the natural and material life; he learns that he is a Divine being, having all the powers that his Father had intended him to have.

This not only makes him a man, but it makes him a priest as well, for he walks with God as did his fathers before him in the long ago.

As he goes onward with the work his judgment becomes clear and this will be the balance between reason and intuition, for the spiritual development must bring with it intuition, that mighty power of the soul.

Reason will determine the use of intelligence on the natural plane, while intuition reveals the light of intelligence on both the natural and spiritual planes. Thus man becomes a twofold being.

Attaining to that clear inner vision sometimes called spiritual perception, and exercising the same intelligently and conscientiously, one's whole character will be permeated with the quality of equity, which is the spiritual side of justice. This judgment faculty regenerated is the mediator between the spiritual and the natural life.

Love, tenderness, goodness, and truth are four great essentials for the development of the Divine or the Christisis in man; and the Divine must dwell within, the Divine must grow, must create, must develop.

CHRISTISIS

What is the Word? It is a fire from heaven, a fire from the world of the soul. It is from the Father. It is life. It is the "Light that lighteth every man that cometh into the world- body- flesh." If man does not accept this light it is his own fault, for if the light is placed before him and he accepts it not, then he has no excuse for failure in this world, no matter whether it be upon the material or the spiritual plane. True success always depends upon both planes and true religion is of both planes.

In order to become that which it was intended for us to be we must keep the Divine Laws in our mind and heart, no matter what the world thinks of us, for we have nothing to fear if we obey these laws and live in harmony with them.

In order to do this neither cant nor creed is necessary. It is only required that we live natural lives, that we harbor neither hate nor thoughts of revenge, that love becomes the ruling power in our characters, that we recognize ourselves to be of the one Universal Creating Power and, as such, Creators upon our plane of being.

Look into the center of your being and you will find there a fire. This is your God- it is the Christisis. The more you recognize this being, the more powerful it becomes until the Great Universal Spirit overshadows you and gives evidence that you are one with that which men call God.

If you endeavor to manifest love and yet continue to think evil or hate, you are simply creating and feeding a serpent which will grow strong. When this serpent becomes developed he will strike you. It is necessary to reject or change all evil thoughts. We should think only that which is good. Evil thoughts, unkind, impatient thoughts are the weeds that choke out all flowers and ruin the garden. Loving, kind, patient thoughts are only transmuted evil thoughts. We suffer from evil because we think evil. When we think evil we suffer more from these thoughts and their results than any one else does. We ourselves drink all the poison that is

CHRISTISIS

produced from the evil vibrations or hate currents in our soul. It is therefore to our own benefit to improve our mode of thinking.

Mind is the creator or destroyer. Control the mind. It is the thing to fear, it will beguile you, watch it.

When we say that we will do a thing with a settled intention to do it, then we are in a positive state of mind. Thought then is powerful and attracts to itself that which is of like quality. We must then be careful, for our thoughts are the magnet that will attract all other thoughts of like kind to us.

To yield the mind to grief, anger or intensity of any kind causes the thoughts to attract its kind; or possibly this yielding of the mind to intensity may submerge the whole consciousness in that particular thought current or wave. This intensity is good, provided it is in a worthy cause and is directed toward the accomplishment of some great and worthy work, but if it is in anger, fear or jealousy, then it is decidedly destructive.

If you want to build up a powerful individuality, a powerful mind and a more powerful soul, then avoid all intense feelings that are closely allied with the passions.

To build, repeat again and again, whenever you think of it, the highest truths that you know. Day by day establish the habit of right thinking and thereby establish a center within yourself which is to become a dynamo of mighty power. When you desire to accomplish any specific work, sit down and think earnestly, quietly, yet confidently, upon the subject. Formulate a picture of that which you desire to accomplish; if you cannot visualize it, at least express it in a word or in a few words and then center all your attention upon the accomplishment of the object in view. This is to be thought of as an exercise in concentration; as one may take breathing exercises or movements in physical culture. At other times one should concentrate his attention upon the duties in

CHRISTISIS

which he is then engaged.

If it be knowledge that you wish to attain, formulate your desire in specific terms, hold your attention exclusively in that line for a time and seek for knowledge that will help you to accomplish your desire. Keep the mind fixed upon that special idea, allow only those thoughts to find place in your mind for the time being and never for a moment doubt your ability to succeed.

It is well to have a special time each day when you can give your entire attention to the thing that you wish to accomplish, focus the mind for ten minutes at a time, gradually increasing the time until you are able to hold your attention upon the thought as long as you desire. It may be difficult at first, but it is with this as with all things else, practice will make perfect. However, the student must not make the mistake of overdoing or of thinking he should do this all the time. Remember that only the listening ear catches the vibrations from the higher realm; only the faithful heart is worthy of revelations from the inmost- the Christisis, only the discreet tongue is able to utter words out of the law.

Always remember that the natural law holds good in the spiritual world, and that the spiritual law holds good in the natural world. We do not teach you a one-sided philosophy, but we teach you the equal development of both the material and the spiritual. We would teach you to succeed not only in the material world but also in the spiritual, and therefore we teach you how to build a soul first, for then all other things will be possible to you.

The success of the true man becomes his religion because true success and religion are one. No success is lasting unless it is founded upon absolute spiritual law, the law as taught by the old masters, each one of whom made his religion his business and his business his religion.

It is one's duty, it is always to one's advantage, to keep at

CHRISTISIS

all times responsive to the infinite intelligence from which one may receive that which will upbuild the life powers, and increase the knowledge of life. This one can do in its fullness only by developing the Christisis within, for thus one's own center becomes responsive at all times to the infinite center of intelligence.

In this mighty work the law of old, "As a man soweth, so shall he also reap," still is law. Whatever thoughts you think, in due time will return to you again, laden with good or ill as the case may be, for each thought that one thinks becomes a part of his attracting power and helps toward success or failure.

As you continue in this mighty work, your faculty of judgment becomes more keenly developed. You become more fully equipped in the use of your faculties on the spiritual basis. In proportion as the natural man is made obedient to the spirit, in that proportion does he become sensitive to the Divine Presence. This process of growth we call the building of the soul or finding of the Christisis.

It is this development and consequent reliance upon the divine that makes man an instrument of the Infinite and qualifies him to be ordained for the Great Ministry. The purpose of creation is to express perfection. Therefore it is the destiny of man, the creation of the divine, to become the perfect expression of {he Creator, in whose image and likeness he is made, and even to become a creator himself.

The process of attainment is the building of the soul or Christisis within. By the use of the faculties developed through this process of growth all desirable things are possible.

This growth refers not only to the things of the spirit or the soul, but to the things of the physical and material as well and it is utterly impossible for the man or woman who has followed these

CHRISTISIS

laws and becomes developed in soul to be a failure.

Develop this power, this being within, this soul; use it in order to attain still more and higher. It is only according to your faith and your work that you will receive.

This is not intellectual apprehension, but a realization of the soul. It is not a mere belief in facts stated by others. Attainment means to know, and true knowledge does not come from without but from the Christisis within.

All life, all love, all power belongs to the soul. When the body has decayed the soul still retains these three qualities, life, love, power. Therefore, you do not build for the present only, but for all eternity.

In teaching you this science we teach you expression not on one plane only, but on every plane of being. This is necessary in order to perfect the individual, and you become not only a personality, but a perfect individuality, if you desire to be such.

CHRISTISIS

LESSON TWO

In beginning the search for wisdom and knowledge the student finds himself wandering here and there, unable to catch the something definite or tangible which his soul hungers for. It is true that he does not recognize that this hunger is of the soul, because he thinks only of his personality, but he does know that he wants something, something he is not able to find. This hunger for something really comes from the soul.

When the word religion is mentioned the would-be philosopher turns away in displeasure. He has had enough experience with religion, he is seeking for knowledge, for something more consistent with his own point of view. He does not know that religion, knowledge and science are really one.

When we mention philosophy to the would-be religionist he affrightedly turns away and flees from the horror of what he believes to be a sacrilegious thought. Why is this? Because neither of these seekers has found the truth, and the real truth weds religion and philosophy in an inseparable bond. Several classes of seekers are found among the people of the world.

There are those seeking they know not what. They are hungry and would be filled, but they know not for what they hunger.

Some think that they want religion. Others think they want philosophy, and still others want science. All these can be satisfied with the one thing, knowledge and development of the powers of the mind and soul, and this knowledge and training will bring them all three, for the three are one. True religion comes from the heart, from the within. True knowledge also comes from within, and the two make up science. The twain are one.

CHRISTISIS

In the search for what he wants, the seeker has but one thing for a guide- that is desire. When he knows what he really desires it is but a matter of time until that desire can be fulfilled, provided he is faithful to the desire.

There are many cults, there are many creeds, many doctrines, so that there seems to be a religion for everybody- a philosophy for everybody.

But he who reaches truth through the inner illumination or soul growth, has neither a special creed nor doctrine, for his religion is a religion-philosophy- science; it is his life; it is a part of him, and not something which he merely believes. He knows.

In the study of cults, creeds, science and doctrines we wander from path to path- wind from one theory or belief (call it what you will) to another, until we find one that seems to harmonize with our mind and thought; then we accept it as the truth. We call it truth because it pleases our own individual self. It is truth to us because it tallies with our view of the truth.

But is it really the truth?

The true seeker must be unbiased, he must seek not a system nor a creed, but a truth, and the truth cannot be found in externals but in internals- it is to be found only through a system of self-development which, like the miner finding gold, the seeker finds within the earth (body).

Now know, that he who truly seeks for the truth or the way to the truth, will not accept because of any self idea, but that he will put all his ideas aside and follow the training and then as he develops, the truth will come to him and he will know the truth. The truth comes from the inner soul, but a path must be made for it to come out over. No creed, doctrine, religion or philosophy can open this path, only a system of true development can accomplish

CHRISTISIS

this. The seeker cannot attain wisdom and knowledge through his own bigoted and conceited idea of truth.

And the student even with a slight degree of enlightenment is capable of recognizing the truth when it is presented to him, no matter in what form- religious or philosophical.

The skilled gem dealer knows the quality and purity of the diamond, no matter what form it wears, when presented to him. It may be in the rough, it may be unpolished and unskillfully cut, but that does not matter, he knows the diamond in spite of flaws when he sees it.

No man can truthfully say that he believes in nothing. He does believe in something. He believes in what he says. He believes in life, he believes in existence. Man, woman, child believes in these positive and divine laws. The most degraded man on earth believes in life, health, joy, peace and harmony though he may believe that these are not for him.

It makes no difference what sort of a life a man is leading, nor how wicked he is mentally, morally or physically, he seeks life, health, joy, peace and harmony after the manner in which he believes it to exist. If he is totally bad he wants life anyway and he wants the best life can give, but he fails to recognize that a true life is a true religion and a bad life is a bad religion. He does not know that the moral code is actually the religious code.

He is in reality seeking truth, God, the divine law and heritage of all men. but he seeks in a perverted sense. He but he seeks only for the self. He forgets that in the limited self there is no power, but only in the universal Self always says, "Hunt that which will satisfy me."

And the hunt for it begins. We have two selves to satisfy.

CHRISTISIS

There is the better self, the higher self, which is the real self, and there is the lower or mortal self, that which lives for a short time and is no more. We are bound to follow the one or the other. We cannot serve two masters. If we seek for self only we may be successful for a time, but the success is not lasting. But if we seek for the good of the real self, then we seek for the universal whole and in this seeking we are building a divine temple, we are building the Christisis.

The true part of man is the soul; his body is extremely useful for it is his temple, it is the mode of being, the vehicle through which he is able to work and to accomplish.

The truth has never been hidden from those who would know and use with wisdom the great laws. But from the ignorant and profane it has been hidden and will always remain hidden, for a Master has said, "Cast not your pearls before swine, lest they trample them under foot."

This is a divine law and no one can open to the eyes of the undeserving the law of wisdom.

But the wise man sees truth in every form, and is able to read it in the hieroglyphs of the Ancients, the astrology of the Chaldeans, the Vedas of the Hindus, or the Records of the Jews.

Religion is nothing in the world but philosophy. It is a system of living, not a system of believing. It had its root and beginning in the philosophy of the Ancients. The philosophy of the Ancients is the religion of the present, but the majority of men simply believe in it, they do not live it. Ancient philosophy is both the origin and the destiny of man. And when we investigate, the deeper we go and the more sincere we become we keep going farther and farther back until we find that there is "nothing new under the sun." We gain by experience and investigation.

CHRISTISIS

Some believe only in that which they can see. They want a material view of the religion or philosophy which they seek. And yet, if they are faithful they can get this view, for when they learn to know that religion, philosophy and science are really a system of being, and not of mere believing, they, through the living will become a new creature. This then will be religion personified; it will be more, it will be success personified and then the seeker will know that in finding religion he has also found success, happiness, health and immortality.

It is such a religion as this that the world demands, it is such a system of culture that enlightened man wants and in the building of the soul, the finding of the Christisis in the temple, he will have found all.

We may not be able to see the life force in any living thing, plant or animal, but we know it has life force, because we can see that it grows. It is the same with success and with religion; we may not be able to see the divine spark, but we can see the growth of him who has it, because he personifies it in himself and in his works. The foolish man is the man who believes only what he sees. And another foolish man is the one who cannot recognize truth wherever found; even when it is perverted, twisted, warped and confounded in the views, theories, reckonings and guesses of self-illusioned teachers, preachers and leaders of the blind.

From the Masters of Egypt came the truth to the western world. Egypt brought forth the philosophy or religion of wisdom and knowledge and it was in Egypt, in the initiation taught there, that man was first taught the mighty secrets of the inner growth, then it was called the Osiris-Isis. In later centuries came Jesus, the Christ, teaching mankind this inner philosophy. He called it "the Kingdom of God which is within you." In the new cycle this perfected inner life will be called the Christisis, because as Jesus, a Master, had promised to return, so is the Christisis now here among men.

CHRISTISIS

It has been taught that the Egyptians worshiped idols and the student must therefore learn that the symbols of the Egyptian religion were not worshiped any more than the Christian worships the paper and ink and the a, b, c that imparts to him the knowledge he seeks in the Scriptures. The symbol was the manner and degree of expression. "We see a picture of a cow. That picture is not the cow itself but it represents the cow. It is the symbol of the cow. It gives us knowledge concerning the cow- what it can do, what it can produce and how it can benefit mankind. It is not the real cow, although it expresses the real."

It is strange that the truths of symbolic religion have been so misunderstood. It is just as sensible to say that we worship the picture of a cow as to say that the symbols of the sun were worshiped in their symbolic form. Naturally, it is to be understood that millions in Egypt may have worshiped the symbols just as there are millions in the world at the present time who worship the image or symbol of Christ and Mary.

All philosophies and religions are based on, and have derived from sun worship their ideas of life, love and existence.

The sun as the sun was never worshiped by the Initiates of Egypt. The Christian religion of today is far more complicated than the worship of the Egyptians and really partakes more of the nature of symbol worship.

We all worship, seek, hunger for the force which sustains the universe- life.

The Egyptians worshiped the Source of Life, the Giver and Receiver of all good from the birth to the death of man.

Is this different from any other worship of today?

But we would do more for the student, we would teach

CHRISTISIS

him not only to worship this source, but to find and develop it within himself. We would show him how to develop this force so that he not only will know it but may also be able to use it. When we do this we teach him no external or arbitrary religion. We teach him a system of living, and this will make him religious. It will make him a philosopher, and it will make him a scientist, for when all things of the earth life have passed away this thing remains with him, it is therefore greater, by far, than any so-called science of earth men. What do you seek? Is it life? Is it success? Is it religion?

We give life, for we may become creators of beings. We sustain life, because we feed it. We crave it, thirst for it, and strive for it for ourselves. This immortal life, the force that generates it and gives it, we call God, the Universal Life.

The Universal Life became dynamic in the individual. The Egyptians called it Osiris because they could not speak the true name of God. We will, in the new time, call it Christisis, because we will not only believe in it, but we will know it, understand it, use it.

Life, wisdom, science, philosophy and religion are all within the soul of man. The soul is the fountain, the life giver. The soul is the power and force of life. The true man, the successful man, the religious man, the scientific man, must know his own soul, and he must recognize its powers and know how to use them.

The student does not praise himself, nor flaunt his wisdom and knowledge before the blinking, unseeing eyes of the profane, self-seeking world. He knows better than that, for he is living the life of the re-generate being.

In the work of obtaining health, success, peace of mind, or whatever you seek, all these things must be taken into consideration, for the student must remember that the very same

CHRISTISIS

law that makes for success in his chosen field, can also give him health, it can give him harmony and peace of mind, and it is bound to be his religion in the true sense. All these things are one and the same thing.

The student learns to understand the power of his mind, then he learns how to use his mind in the development of that higher and greater power within himself, the soul, the immortal part of his nature. And as he accomplishes this work, illumination is the result, and this is the great power that will enable him to obtain all things needful. Gradually the result of such a training becomes habit; and the great thing to do is to establish right habits in the thought world. It does not require a long time to establish right habits; not even right habits of thought. When correct thought attitude is established then right thinking and consequently right building of character become habitual and man builds a mighty and powerful body, mind and soul before he is aware of having accomplished so great a work.

CHRISTISIS

LESSON THREE

Life is concentration. Concentration is accumulation. Through concentration of thought we accumulate that upon which we concentrate and in that way we become a mighty magnetic center for the attraction and accumulation of that which we desire.

In this great work we naturally think of the student as desiring all that is good and pure, for we believe that he recognizes the fact that, after having found the soul and having become illuminated, he will receive other things that he may need or desire.

It was for this reason that the Master of old said, "Seek ye first the kingdom of heaven, and all else will be added unto you."

This is true, for by seeking the kingdom of heaven we seek illumination of soul, and when that is obtained we have become clear sighted and intuitive. Illumination of soul is the greatest experience man can have, and through this power it is possible in time to obtain all the other things that we may desire.

The building of a soul means also illumination of soul, and with this comes the regeneration of the body. The student will therefore clearly understand that a deceased body is an impossibility when the soul is illuminated, because true development is threefold. It is of the body, the mind and the soul. It elevates all three and the three become one in unity.

As a result of this spiritual unfoldment or regeneration of life, the soul comes into a new consciousness, that is, spiritual consciousness. The possibilities of such a soul are unlimited. Even the possibilities upon the material plane become unlimited. The development of these spiritual powers bring with them a judgment that is good and this judgment gives the power to adjust conditions

CHRISTISIS

in their natural and proper order.

The student will thus clearly understand that with this illuminated soul, with this spiritual understanding, he may accomplish the things that would otherwise be impossible.

The spirit of man is divine, it is that which he brings with him to the great world of action. It will become, as he accumulates, the connecting link between his body and his soul. It is an offspring from the great invisible manifestation. It is always connected with its source and it will help to bring the soul to its Father.

Mind has two aspects, active and passive. The rational faculty is the intellect which is continually active, gathering knowledge through reason or study; it is that which believes but which has no way of knowing except by believing the authority of others. Intuition, the highest power of man, which can come only through soul or spiritual illumination, is the receptive faculty; it can receive knowledge direct and without conscious reasoning. It knows because that which it receives comes from within, from itself, from that great temple God said dwelt within us.

When the student understands that there is a spiritual plane in man which is far more reliable than any outward plane, he will seek this inner consciousness and receive therefrom true knowledge.

With this building of the soul the light from the universal soul, the Father of Christisis, will begin to flood his soul so that he will understand how to use his mental faculties, and he will thus be able to control conditions on the spiritual and on all lower planes.

Thus will the student gradually come to understand that he is working in a circle. While in the state in which practically all

CHRISTISIS

mankind live, which is called the natural state, he blindly follows the laws of being upon that piano yet gradually, as he uses his thoughts consciously for the building of a real spiritual soul and as that soul becomes illuminated, in short, as lie finds the Christisis within himself, be is also building a powerful mind. And so, while he builds an illuminated soul, the illuminated soul in return builds a mighty mind, and the two help to build a powerful body. This is Being- upon the threefold plane and man becomes what the Gods had intended him to be. Just in proportion as he raises his consciousness to the Spiritual Invisible Center, in that proportion will be the illumination of his soul. This illumination becomes the light that will lead him onward and upward to greater and grander things.

He who has attained even a slight degree of soul consciousness has already connected with the Universal Father of Light and has found not only Christisis within himself to that degree but he is already in conscious touch with God and finds his life in Him. Just in proportion as he does this, in that proportion will this great spiritual power control his life as a rational being in a material world.

All Masters, in all times, have taught the few that they are the children of God and that all the power that has been given to the few will be given to the many, provided they prepare a place within themselves in which this Divine Being may live.

You cannot live an irrational life and expect to entertain the Godhead, and you cannot live the life of the material flesh and still be the temple of Christisis. In order to be- come the temple of Christisis you must become truly a man. To become such you must rid the mind of all such thoughts as these of hate, jealousy, fear, revenge; for these do not belong to the spiritual or rational man. These thoughts belong to the beast nature within man and not to his God nature.

CHRISTISIS

What then is necessary? It is simply necessary that you shall examine yourself carefully, find out the undesirable tendencies of thought and the weak points within yourself, ask yourself whether these really belong to the rational man and the answer to you will be that they do not. Then place before yourself the ideal of transmuting these unnatural qualities of your being. Recognize the fact that these base passions do not give you strength, but lead to weakness. Recognize the fact that good feeling towards all mankind brings power, that love to all creatures brings power. As the Father has said that all are His children, realize that you also can be a son of God in very truth, and that you can therefore prepare a place in your heart for the coming Messiah. You prepare for the Messiah by cultivating the attitude of love.

Recognize the fact that you can be in the world even while you are bringing these changed conditions about. Recognize the fact that improving one's thoughts does not take any pleasure or possibilities from one, but that it continually enhances and intensifies the joys and possibilities of life, bringing one greater peace of mind, greater pleasure, greater health and greater possibilities.

Thus will you, gradually, change from an unnatural life to a natural one, and this change also brings you a new consciousness, for little by little you come to know that there is something within you which you had not previously recognized. You will find that there is a voice, the cry of a babe, within, constantly calling you and asking you to listen. That is the awakening soul; it is the Christisis which will bring you to all things. Thus, by heeding this voice and obeying the dictates of the soul, in due time, will you have changed from an unnatural being to a perfectly natural or normal one with all spiritual possibilities become dynamic.

Man, as he lives today, thinks that the only happiness is in

CHRISTISIS

the gratifying of his senses, in having all his thoughts, feelings, desires and sensations in the physical being. He forgets that any difficulty in the physical organism diminishes his ability to enjoy even the pleasures of the physical being. To be limited to the physical plane or to be a slave to physical pleasures is not the natural or the normal life.

The person who is bound by this unnatural limitation ignores everything that may be upon a higher plane and he cannot recognize any better life and so long as he lives in that state of mind he cannot rise to any other plane.

It is therefore necessary that the student should first understand what it is to live a normal, natural life, and then understand the power of thought. In this he has taken the first great step that will lead him to all that is good and true, while still not being deprived of happiness or greater possibilities.

The student may have been taught that to lead a pure life brings suffering and pain with it, but he forgets that living an unnatural life also brings great pain and sorrow. He does not consider that practically the whole lifetime of man, with the exception of a few moments of pleasure now and then, is spent in pain or in sorrow.

There may be trials for him who tries to live the normal or spiritual life, but he must remember that the greatest trials and struggles, the hardest battles really lead us to glory and higher attainment, if we but stand to win. The great test comes when we are tempted, mocked, and everything seems to go wrong. There is no test in living a good life when everything goes right.

How different is it in the world of pure sense? In the sense life there are also bitter trials, bitter sorrows and extreme pain, but instead of bringing higher attainment and greater power, they simply bring weakness.

CHRISTISIS

The student will thus see the great difference between the sense life and the spiritual life; the immense gulf that separates the two. On the one side is pain and suffering, but leading to power and attainment. On the other side is pain, sorrow and suffering, but leading to weakness instead of power.

To be possessed of self-control, (and this comes with illumination,) is to lead to high attainments. If the soul is cleansed it will be able to bless those who oppose it; it will know how to forgive them in their ignorance, for the soul recognizes that these oppositions are not blocks to its own progress- but rather tests of its strength, and therefore they are of the greatest help to attainment. Tests of strength should be thought of as opportunities for developing strength.

Manifest that which you love. You will do that anyhow, for if your life is one of trickery, though you may try to hide this tendency yet every movement of your being, every act- even that which would seem to be one of love- shows that it is trickery that you really love.

If you love that which is good you may try to hide your deeds from the world, but the world will feel the vibrations in which you live and gradually come to honor you.

All great men have become such by concentration of one purpose upon the object which they desired to accomplish. Singleness of thought is like a sun glass which, being held to one point a sufficient length of time, kindles a fire in the things that obstruct the light, until a hole is burned through dark matter to the source of light and heat.

When the flame is kindled you will know that you have a soul within you. You will know that the Christisis is in process of formation, the embryonic state. The next effort is to get within it, to blend and become one in mind and soul. When in the soul,

CHRISTISIS

which is love, you are in God and in time may become like unto God; but the process of gestation is slow.

This is the process of self-development or illumination and time is required, but all may accomplish this who are truly willing to reach the highest on all planes of being.

The great center of thought is in the nerve ganglion or network of nerves known as the Solar Plexus, just above the back of the stomach. The effect that true concentration of thought will have on you as a person or individualized identity will be a warm feeling in this center and this gentle heat or flame will become a ranting flame until the vibratory forces are so strong that it fills the whole body with intense heat and the dew of heaven is felt upon the brow, the;more you concentrate the greater the falling of dew until it is like a summer shower.

These intense vibrations, like wireless waves, are in connection with all other vibrations of like nature and this explains why it is possible for us to become that which we truly will to be and possible for us to obtain the things that we really desire to obtain. Herein is the whole law.

There is also a center from which ideas are evolved, and this center is developed in harmony with the great center mentioned above. Thus, all centers in our being are developed when we develop the one great center just as the planets and stars evolve in their circle in harmony with the sun.

The student will therefore easily understand that if he hates any one he is developing the center of hate and that all other centers in his being will develop with this center. The same law governs the development of the love center, the center of justice, the center of genius and all other centers, for all conditions have a center within man just as every planet and star in the heavens has a circle of action and influence. If we develop the love center, the

CHRISTISIS

vibrations of love come to us with words of instruction, and we know that God is love as well as wisdom.

Love and truth- Christisis- are one; infinite, unlimited freedom, but being divided in the soul, love is hungry for truth- Christisis- or in love with it, and keeps searching for what it desires. The soul sends out from itself forces, as telegrams, in order to obtain a reply. In order to receive an answer to its quest the soul opens a receiver in the mind, a cell or womb into which the answer comes as thought which germinates into ideas. This empty reservoir, which opens as a flower into which the universe may deposit itself, may be called the ideal center, the center which evolves ideas. We are fed from this center with truth, if we are in search for truth. This is the place where telegrams from the infinite meet the listening ear, and intellect and perception are born of the light radiating from the infinite. If yon make your centers positive, desiring only the truth and that which is good, then you will receive truth only, and gradually the messages that you receive in the soul will become more and more positive until you come into conscious touch, through intuition, with all that is.

What is love? Love seeketh not its own. Love is God; it is a radiance, a warming, drawing power (magnetism), attracting us on and on to perfection; radiating on us, through us, around us.

Manifest that which you love, bring forth the thing you love. You love what you bring forth or manifest. Learn to love- learn to bring forth or manifest only that which is true and good and great, for as you do this so will imperial and glorious power come to you.

If you are illuminated by the light of love in your emotional nature, you are inspired by the true feeling which will find expression in the thoughts and actions that are true and good. This action will be of the spirit, and you may trace it to the spirit of love, the soul, which is in sympathy with all that is good and

CHRISTISIS

true.

Why was man placed upon earth? The destiny of man, or of the soul in man, is to express the heavenly, that which is of the Father, through the earthly. It is therefore essential that knowledge concerning the divine and every step of progress necessary should be known by man. When he knows this all things are possible to him.

In the accumulation of good we become one with God and therefore a part of Him, which places us into sonship. Therefore, by making the weak points strong and the strong ones still stronger, we can reach the highest; we will be able to find the Christisis.

There is but one way- the way of Christisis- the coming Savior.

Watch the mind. Control its thoughts. They will deceive you. Listen to the voice of consciousness (soul knowledge), it is the guide (angel). Give heed to the awakening of ideas, thoughts, light, the soul of gods who are manifested to the soul receiving sight and illumination. Mind is the builder of the soul- of Christisis.

CHRISTISIS

LESSON FOUR

The undeveloped soul within man is like the seed planted in the ground, capable of growing. Some seeds spring up but are crushed back into earth; some push through the earth and become beautiful flowers in the garden of the gods.

The soul holds within itself the essence of the Creator of man, the world and all flesh.

This divine essence of life is the spark from which to develop the Christisis. It creates life and sustains all life. No one can deny the existence of life. No one can deny the creating power of life, and no one can deny its force.

That life is creator of man is the true Esoteric teaching of the Masters. The ancient Masters did not recognize God as a person. They did not worship God as a being apart from the one supreme divine life, but as the one life in all things, as the principle of good, as the life giver, the Creator. The beautiful in all its forms and phases was recognized as being identical though designated by different names in conformity and harmony with the Supreme Creator of the beautiful. We have mind, heart, soul and body.

We make gods of mind, heart, soul, body and the so-called gods of the Ancients were simply the names given to mind, heart, soul, body and the flesh. The real Masters always taught the one God. They taught that God is the Supreme Being. They taught one Savior and this Savior is the Christisis, the developed being within us, the God which is in the temple.

These gods of the ancients were parts of the whole- the governing soul of all from which all sprung and which all contains.

CHRISTISIS

"I am yesterday, today and tomorrow, for I am born again and again. I am that whose force is manifest and nourisheth the dwellers in the West. I am the guides in the East. The Lord of the two forces who seeth by His own light. The Lord of resurrection who cometh forth from the dusk and whose birth is from the house of death."

"Ye two divine hawks upon your station; watchers of the material world; ye who go with the bier to its eternal home, and you who conduct the ship to the sun; advancing onward from the highest heaven to the place of the sarcophagus."

"This is the Lord of the shrine which standeth in the center of the earth, He is in me; and I am in Him."

"In Him we live and move and have our being."

It is the same today as in the fore-time. These extracts from the "Book of the Dead", of the Egyptians are very similar to those from the Bible, the book of the Christian. This book was in existence, was an old book 3733 B.C. From this we see that the Egyptian faith or religion, or philosophy was the "shrine," the center or creator of all religions or philosophies that have ever existed. From the Egyptians we have learned of God.

From the Egyptians we have learned all the laws of being, all the evolutions and developments of mind, soul and body.

From the religion of Christisis we will now learn the mysteries and greater development of the soul, the highest that there is, the highest that man can know or be. For Christisis includes all that can be found in the soul, and in the soul is all that there is or can be.

What is God? Who is He? Where is He?

CHRISTISIS

All nations, all creeds, all philosophies agree that He is the Father of Light, He is life, He is love. Light, life and love, if understood, would give the wisdom and knowledge of the gods. There are those who ask us, "Who are the gods?"

The gods are those who have perfected the soul life, who have overcome the world and all flesh and are in conscious and supreme harmony and union with the Father. Then there are beings who have never been born into the earth life, the flesh, but who are pure, perfect and molded in the image of the Father.

All these are of the One Supreme Ruler, living in conscious harmony with His laws- controlling, guiding and assisting in the shaping of events and the destiny of empires and mankind. All nations, all laws, all humanity are under control of these great souls who are ever watching to assist and protect those who reach out for help and who are struggling to overcome the flesh and the world. These are the gods which the heathens are supposed to have engraved in stone. They are supposed then to have worshiped the stone as a god.

That the heathen literally worshiped stone is not true. Did the Hebrews worship the tablets of stone or the law and truths of the commandments? Do the Christians worship the water they baptize with or the idea of the birth of the spirit? All creeds agree that God is the Father of light, of life, of love, but none of them know what that light is, what that life is, or what that love is.

The awakening of the Christisis within you will teach you all things; the emblems of Christianity remain the same, but we teach you the Spirit, not the law merely.

Where is God? Where are the gods? "Ye are the temples of the living God," has come down to us in thundering tones and the Christisis not only tells you this, but tells you how to find God. Love is the creator of all. The creator of light and life. Love is the

CHRISTISIS

life of God- the fire that creates being and beings. No mere theologist or creed believer can know God, nor where He is.

He is the "Lord of the shrine which standeth in the center of the earth. He is in me; and I am in Him."

"I shine forth as the Lord of Light and life and the glorious law of light."

The science of Christisis teaches you how to find this light, and when you find the light, then you will know that "He is in you; and you in Him."

Did the ancient priests and philosophers know this?

They did or they would never have been able to teach mankind the most mighty philosophy ever known.

Why, then, did not they teach all nations?

Why does not God teach all nations?

The great truths have been taught from all times to the few who were willing to receive them and follow them. "Pearls cannot be thrown before swine," nor can great truths be taught to the undeserving. The truth can be taught to those only who are really willing to receive; and even to receive the truth is not sufficient; the student must live the truth if he would learn to know the power of the truth.

God is wisdom and only the wise learn wisdom.

It is not enough to learn about God- we must learn to know God. We must find Him. When we learn what He is, through the development and awakening of the soul, then we know what He is and where He is. Man is the ruler and maker of his destiny.

CHRISTISIS

He is of God. He is made in the image of God, and God rules and will always rule. Man proceeded from God and may return to God. If he does not become like unto God with His creating powers then it is his own fault, for God has placed within him all the powers, or rather, the spark from which he may develop all the powers that belong to God, after whose image man was made.

God does not cease to exist. He is everlasting, and all things that come, from Him may be everlasting. It is within the power of man to choose his own destiny.

When we truly realize our relationship to God we will realize our supremacy over flesh and all its illusions.

God is not Father over religious matters alone; He is the good of all things, no matter whether it be spirituality, health, success, happiness, or all that is great. Therefore, he who is most like unto God has most of His powers. It therefore follows that the development of the Christisis within us will give us the power of God.

All that is mortal must die- all that is immortal will live and that which is mortal has no power over that which is immortal. The weaker cannot control the stronger- nor the less the greater.

The body cannot control the mind. The mind controls the body. "What we think and how we think, draws us into the realm or plane of the illusions of the senses or away from the senses.

If we think right we will build right and no law of evil can prevail against us.

The material around us has no power over us when we realize and acknowledge the supremacy of the spiritual- the soul over matter.

CHRISTISIS

The soul is the real man. The soul is the father of man, the maker and sustainer of all that is. God is simply the greater soul. The soul of man is a miniature of the greater soul, a child of the supreme soul with all its powers and possibilities but in a lesser degree.

Soul is all that lives, and if we do not develop soul then there is nothing to live and it will not matter what faith we hold or to what creed we subscribe. Unless we develop the soul, find the Christisis within us, then there is nothing to live forever. Soul is the essence of life. It is that which sustains life, and the more of soul we have and the greater its development, the more of real life will we have.

Soul is light, it is the divine image- fire. Man is in the image of God, but the developed soul is the divine, the fire image, of God.

The vital spark of the soul is in every human being, but it will depend upon the human being himself whether the soul is to live forever or to die. Soul is God made and for that reason it may become all powerful. God made man, man did not make himself. God gave the vital spark of the soul, but He gave man the privilege to develop it or to let it die.

Many past philosophies and religions have erred because they taught and believed that man was something apart from God- that he is sufficient unto himself- his illusioned, mortal flesh-loving self. And after making himself in his own image man attempts to make God in the image he conceives Him to be.

Man's conception of God is not true because his conceptions through wrong living have become clouded and totally unreliable.

As man learns that there is a God and that he has been

CHRISTISIS

made in God's image and that the vital spark of immortality is within himself and that he may, if he wills, develop this spark into the Christisis, his vision will clear, and he will see and know God as He is.

Is it any wonder, then, that the God men have blindly worshiped has failed them? Is it any wonder that the real God will not conform to the rule, law and thought that mortal man in his ignorance and stupidity has endeavored to make for Him? God will not conform to the laws made or held by man. Man must conform to and obey the laws of God.

The trouble all came through wrong thinking, through wrong beliefs, through thinking that man can be saved by believing. Man can save himself only through right living, through the development of that vital spark of immortality which God has planted within him.

God has never turned and will never turn from man; man turned away from God and His just laws. God is always the same, His laws are the same. Man is not the same, he is constantly changing. Just as long as man allows his body to rule, allows the desires of the flesh to usurp the desires of the spiritual self and the mind to be clogged with lust and evil imaginings and desires, just that long will he continue to turn away from the center of light, of life, of love and of great achievement.

Merely to say a thing will not remove the cause of evil unless one does what lie says. To believe in immortality; will not make one immortal. To believe in success, even though one has a successful plan or system, will not bring success; it is only in living one's plan that he will be able to succeed.

You may say that you worship God, you may go through the proper formula, but unless you live the worship you are not worshiping in truth but only in the form. Immortality can be yours

CHRISTISIS

only as you worship God in spirit and in truth.

You cannot live the life and still think thoughts of lust, evil, and self. You cannot hate your neighbor and be a true servant of God at the same time. Unless you serve the One in whose image you are, you cannot become immortal, you cannot build the divine image, you cannot be permanently successful.

Religion and science, religion and success, (that is true success,) are one and the same thing; it is the Christisis.

You cannot covet anything that is your neighbor's and serve God at the same time. You are serving the flesh when you covet. You yield to illusions, for the flesh has no true power, it is only temporary. Flesh is not the real man and that which seems to be success is but temporary and fleeting.

Soul is the real man. Soul is the thing that suffers, feels, knows. Soul is of the divine spirit- it is God, and it is within every man, woman and child. To conform to the coming Messiah, He that is now but newly born, we call the awakened soul, the Christisis.

It is all that there is. The flesh has no power. It is helpless, dull, lifeless, without soul. When the soul has left the body, the body is dead. The soul, if it has found the light, the divine center, will live on throughout eternity, it was successful.

Every materialist, mentalist and spiritualist must admit the truth of these statements. When the soul leaves the body, the body is dead, The soul lives, even the most orthodox admit this. If soul is the only real part of man and is the only part of man that lives after so-called death, then soul is all that is of permanent value; soul in man, the divine spark from God the oversoul, the life of all there is.

CHRISTISIS

Man's soul, woman's soul, both are from God and are a part of God. The flesh is the manifestation of soul- it is the temple of the soul- hence in reality all belongs to soul. There is nothing that lives and moves, that creeps, that grows, outside of this influence. God always loves. He is Love. He is the Fire of life, the Soul of being.

It is this greater life that we teach the student. It is this great law which we would have him live. For if he does so, then he will develop the mighty soul within himself, and he will become immortal, a master in material things as in spiritual things.

The lure of the flesh and the illusion of sin and all lusts and all covetousness may attract for a time, but they are not real. They are the vampires that do not really exist, for they have no life except that which they sap from mankind.

Only the divine soul or image is permanent. This is what man really is, always was and always will be. Illusion is not the real man. The senses and the lusts of covetousness, greed, spite, jealousy, envy and the like are not real. When man lives in the senses he is living a transient, imaginary, unreal existence. All temptations of the flesh are but illusions, snares. The soul is never tempted- it is the senses that are tempted. The soul will struggle against all the evils and illusions of the world. Even the worldly grow weary and disgusted with the transitory pleasures and illusions the world offers them.

How many have in desperation tried to stifle the cry of the awakening soul life, the soul which cried out against sin and illusion? But when the soul cried out they grew weary. The pleasures turned into ashes, and the worm-eaten rose fell from its stem. To find the soul is to live. To really live is to be both successful and immortal. To become immortal is to become like unto God.

CHRISTISIS

LESSON FIVE

The whole external universe is the outpicturing of the thoughts retained within the infinite soul.

God first had the picture of the universe in His mind, and then from these thoughts held by the infinite mind He built the universe. In the same manner was man, in the divine image, made. He was given all the powers held by the infinite mind and soul, though in a lesser degree. For this reason can man become the creator of worlds and conditions, but on a limited scale.

That which is good is never lost. When we realize that all that God made is good we realize that all good is eternal, immortal, and is retained, but all outside of good is not retained in the good. When consciousness becomes introspective or interior, the inner vision may see soul images, which either have not yet been externalized, or which, having become externalized, have passed from the external plane. The soul is the mirror and image of everything tenable, real, immutable, that transpires or takes place. As for example, books have been written that may have been destroyed, yet the ideas which they expressed, and even the forms of the expression still remain in the interior soul world and it is these images which the developed soul, the Christisis, can open and come into touch with, and receive knowledge from, through the divine gift of intuition, the master passion of the soul.

God is Soul- universal Soul- the universe or world is His body. Everything is imaged in the soul of God, otherwise it could not exist. The soul of God is the universal mirror of God and reflects or retains or images every idea expressed by the soul of God, the Christisis. This is the interior world, the universal world which is the universal soul.

The mind, therefore, that withdraws itself from the

CHRISTISIS

external, and becomes, through the training which we here teach you, consciously active in the inner realm, may perceive, through the divine gift of intuition, and thus may appropriate and re-express the ideas or types of soul images, which are indestructible. This explains why many an inspiring speech, poem or invention may be uttered or given to the world in the same form or expression as that which voiced it in ages past. It explains why the same truth may be expressed in various forms, according to the individual channels through which it passes.

The student will thus perceive why it is possible to make a far greater success in the material world after going through this training than would otherwise be possible. And besides this, while he undergoes this training he comes into conscious touch with the true religious-science world and he becomes a religious master at the same time that he becomes a master of his soul.

Thus understanding this great law, we can say with the Ancient Masters, that "there is nothing new under the sun." As the external man breathes the same air, eats the same food, yet uses what he appropriates according to his individuality, (if he is fortunate enough to have built one,) so does the spiritual man, while using the same thought substance, while being subject to the same universal soul influences, appropriate the ideas and express them according to his individuality. This explains the differentiation of all soul expression.

The greater knowledge brings the greater light, and with every ascending step in the ladder of perfection there is an increased understanding of the infinite soul, because the student becomes more harmonious, and therefore is better able to receive vibrations from the infinite soul.

This understanding of the universal law and the complexity yet simplicity of living in this light, the light inherent in every soul, the light which brings revelations of God, can be

CHRISTISIS

had only by building the soul through the power of the mind, this building must always result in the Christisis, the Son of Man and of God, the two in one.

This light- this Christisis- intelligence awakening in the consciousness, illuminates all things, and is, as it were, like a universal sea, in which souls exist as souls, and from which they may imbibe all knowledge. Those who have gone through this illumination are said to belong to the Church of Divine Illumination, because they are illuminated souls.

This wonderful sea of intelligence or light, like rivers running in all directions, has many channels or currents, but all leading to the one great sea.

These thought rivers contain thought images on all subjects. For example, all thought imaging fear forms a river with the quality of fear predominant. Fear, however, is unreal. It is not indestructible- it is subject to destruction and change. It is transitory; it is undesirable. Therefore it cannot be truth, but it can be changed or transmuted into truth.

Fear is an illusion which the mortal endeavors to convey to the soul, but it is sooner or later recognized as unreal and transitory, something undesirable. All thoughts representing love, truth, praise, joy, gladness, constitute the river of light, whose quality is joyous. This is the divine or infinite source or soul and the river goes on forever. "For men may come, and men may go, But I go on forever."

Positive, bright, happy thoughts are like sunny, sparkling streams, invigorating and buoyant, and it is your duty to come into touch with this stream for it will mean health and youth to you.

Poetry, art, science, religion, all have as many streams in the universal ocean, as there are differentiated classes of thought

CHRISTISIS

on these subjects. God contains only the positive, true, everlasting thoughts for He is the creator. The earth, His spouse, contains all the negative thoughts and that is why the undeveloped earth man is negative, hateful, spiteful, jealous, revengeful and inclines toward all other thoughts that are evil and negative. These negative thoughts exist only on earth, and cannot reach the Godhead, but so long as they are held by man they will govern man. It is the duty of the student to become positive, to raise himself, through development and soul building, to the great ocean of divine religion and science and to bathe in its currents of true, loving, beautiful, health-inspiring thoughts.

The physical, mortal man thinks that evil brings him pleasure, good and truth. This idea is an illusion of the flesh. It is a negative and dark thought and produces currents of muddy, thick, polluted water which brings disease, sorrow, misery and want.

Whosoever is susceptible to fear of any type, will attract to himself the fear that belongs to his type- fear of accident, for example, or of sickness, or death, and he may also become submerged in the fear current of the thought ocean. On the contrary, whoever formulates and holds happy thoughts, will ally himself with the thought currents of happiness or courage or knowledge, according to the quality of his thoughts.

It is for this reason that the general in the army who is fearless will stand in the center of the field, bullets flying all around him, hundreds of his soldiers falling at his very feet, and will himself remain untouched by bullet or sword.

This may be the reason why the man who, tired of life, rushes into all kinds of danger in order to be killed, emerges without harm. He desires to die, he courts death, but he does not fear it.

This may also explain why the promising young man,

having many opportunities before him, is suddenly stricken by some disease or some accident befalls him, and he is ushered into eternity. He fears that he may not live to enjoy the good things before him. Cast out fear. Build the soul of conscience, and know that if you do your part, if you build a soul of love and trust, you will be given all the time that you require in order to accomplish your work.

Do you want understanding on any special subject? Then open your soul to the influx from the thought river containing such knowledge. Seek its fountainhead, the supreme source. Put your question definitely, withdraw all thought from the physical self or external world and become still; that is, cease thinking just as you become quiet and wait for an answer, when you have asked a question of a friend who stands by your side. In the interior stillness, wherein is to be heard the soul voice and the interpretation of things in the ideal world, you will receive the answer; if not in that moment, in a similar one at another time, for you should have a special hour each day when you hush the flesh desires and worship or seek in the spirit.

You are asking your question of infinite soul or intelligence. This brings omnipresent knowledge into your mind in such form as will best appeal to your understanding. "Peace be still, and the wind ceased and there was a great calm."

David said, "Be still and know that I am God."

You have the ability to be still; this ability grows by development and enables you to receive the intelligence. It may be conveyed to you as a feeling, a wordless understanding, or by a vision or image, which is symbolic of the idea to be conveyed. If you do not understand it at first, wait also for understanding. Even though you are unanswered for days, keep the mind receptive toward the subject and explanation will come. The interpretation will be given as you are ready to receive it, and thus will you

CHRISTISIS

begin the practical life in the thought realm. You will learn that in the interior world there is nothing to keep you from receiving what you are ready to appropriate, whether it be knowledge or power, patience, courage, or any gift of the spirit, You will perceive that you are living on a new foundation, that of the soul. You are learning the language of soul, and all the various experiences which come to the soul will enlighten you and add to your knowledge of the law. You will also begin to realize that on the soul plane spiritual qualities exist and that they form connection links between you and God, between you and all souls. You will learn to know that true religion, like science, is something to know, to understand, and not something to believe. You will know that religion means to live and not merely to believe, it is not a creed but a system of living.

In proportion as you appreciate and feel the depth and greatness of this spiritual quality it will become manifest in your individuality. Remember that as you develop these powers, you will have a new system of understanding, you will have a new teacher, you will have a messenger direct from the universal intelligence. This messenger may be called Intuition.

Spiritual quality is but the radiation of God's love in the soul. When this radiation is consciously recognized (as it is after a sufficient degree of soul development), it makes the character spiritual; for the vibrations of God's love breathe into that character all the tendencies and graces which love alone can bestow. To covet earnestly the best gifts is first of all to covet the supreme love that radiates from God; for this is the foundation of all good gifts and makes life the expression of the divine.

You can see that not until self is lost or set aside can soul predominate in life and character. Man made God to suit his mortal belief. He limited God, but God never limited man. God made man after His own likeness, "in His image made He him," and man in his realm is in reality limitless and boundless as God is

CHRISTISIS

in His universe. Man has limited himself by following false beliefs, false creeds, false gods. These false ideas must be set aside, he must recognize his divine heritage, and when he does so he will in truth become a creator, made in the image of God.

The experiences that come to one who is seeking to establish his life on this foundation will be many and diverse. They will affect his life on the threefold planes of being, physical, mental and moral. On the physical plane he will meet with opposition, with menacing conditions. It is for him to overcome opposition, and change that which has the semblance of opposition, to positive affirmation of good, truth, and soul supremacy. The effect which any experience has upon us depends upon our own attitude of mind toward it. If we are determined to extract good from every condition, we find that so-called misfortunes become blessings in disguise.

On the mental plane the student will find much to depress his mind and to deflect his aims. It will be for him to conquer depression, and to make his moral purpose high and holy and powerful; for, the more trials he meets and the more he overcomes the greater will be his strength. This can be accomplished only by realizing the nature of his real being, by taking his stand on the spiritual basis. In his soul, which is the offspring of God, there is omniscience- all knowledge; omnipotence- all power; and omnipresence- all presence. But much training is necessary to enable the student to realize the divine element in his own soul.

As a spiritual being, therefore, he knows not only abstract truth, but relative truth. He can say, "I know, for the knowledge that I have comes not from books, nor from the authority of men, but direct from the universal soul, through the mighty medium of intuition, for I have developed the Christisis within me – I know."

Man is soul, created in the image of the Supreme. Soul. He may express the spirit knowledge and power if only the soul

CHRISTISIS

awakens and claims his divine birth and inheritance. In the midst of relative conditions to assume spiritual knowledge, is the first step toward adjusting conditions. By so doing man is merely acting upon this basis that the soul is the real being, the immortal and the perfect "I" that which was, is, and will be.

This inner being, this Christisis, is not subject to any earthly condition, hence it may say, "I am Master. As Master I direct, govern and change all undesirable relations and conditions. As soul I know, as soul I have all the graces and gifts of the Father, I live in the Father as the Father lives in me." One becomes master of external conditions only by mastering his own thought-kingdom and living the Christ-love, the Christ-truth, the Christ-power.

This is what we mean when we tell you of the soul basis, the only true basis that there is.

You can see how it is that, although you may meet with obstacles on the physical plane, yet having knowledge of the power of soul, your wisdom will enable you to control and wisely master unsatisfactory conditions. You will understand the transitory illusions and temptations of the flesh and will know how to banish them.

Soul, being superior to all, may overcome and banish all that is undesirable. If you acknowledge your spiritual power you will win the victory over every temptation.

Soul wisdom brings understanding, and you are able to deal with what is commonly called your lower nature as with a child that needs training and discipline. Yet having not only the wisdom, but the love inherent in the spirit, you will neither severely condemn nor harshly criticize, but will at all times have the patience, yet firmness which wisdom alone can give. It is a great mistake for the student to feel impatient even with his own shortcomings.

CHRISTISIS

Love is not only the redeeming and re-generating power, but is that which makes for perfection. He who has in his soul love, although invisible, will finally make manifest the fruits of love, which is the visible perfect character of soul. This is the Christisis.

In love there is no condemnation, there is no partiality, there is no evil, there is no limitation, there is no respect of person. To find that love which is of God, is to find the light that shall shine upon you and mate glorious your own real nature. It is the mighty Christisis, the developed, conscious soul.

In the morning and at night, let your first and last thoughts be of the Supreme Divinity, in which you live and move, and have your being. Live continually in the shining light of this thought:

"I realize that my body is created in the image of the Father who is the Light of the World. I realize that my soul, as it develops, will be in the image of the universal soul which is pure light. I know that I can become the creator instead of being the plaything of men and of my own passions, and I know that I can become the Master, the Christisis. the consciously developed soul which will be in touch with the divine Creator, through the glorious gift of intuition."

No words, however harsh, will hurt you; no discord will move you from your serenity; and whether you speak or are silent, whether you sleep or are awake, the power of your spirit and your consciousness will be felt and known as a light to those who sit in darkness. If for a time you lose your lofty outlook, the remembrance of your soul power, recall yourself quickly; fly to the rock, which is your only foundation, His all encircling presence. Let the light of love grow within you, seek the radiance of the light of the soul, become the Christisis.

CHRISTISIS

LESSON SIX

That great Master of Mysticism, Jacob Boehme, said: "God introduces His will into nature for the purpose of revealing His power in light and majesty to constitute a kingdom of joy."

The will is a lever that lifts in any desired direction. Yet it may also be a power that decides the direction. It is the great factor in human experience, which makes or mars character, and fulfills or defeats every promise of nature. Unguided, except by the caprice of the senses, it is the unworthy helmsman that steers the ship directly on the rocks. But exalted, trained, and consecrated through powerful soul development, it leads into the harbor of peace, power and safety.

So subtle and wonderful is this grand faculty, that only the closest study and most careful analysis will reveal either its nature, its modes or action, or its possibilities. From the standpoint of ordinary human experience, it is forceful and sometimes violent, yet always successful in the accomplishment of its ends.

There are two aspects to every force; one is the positive, the other is the negative. Sometimes this duality which runs through everything is called masculine and feminine. Masculine corresponds to the positive, feminine to the passive or negative.

The masculine is always the aggressive, pushing, active, positive power. The feminine is the passive, receptive, hidden, unmanifested potency. Both are requisite to the operation and fulfillment of any project, but either may be too much in excess, thereby causing a lack of balance between the two, and a consequent defeat of the end to be attained. As to will, it is too often only the masculine phase, which is recognized or brought into activity. Will in the sense-man means what is commonly called brute force, because it is the same exhibition of violent

CHRISTISIS

energy directed by will as that seen among animals, the wild beast attacking his prey, or defending his little ones. This is really not will, but simply animal force.

Masculine will force is powerful, but convulsive and short lived; hence while it may accomplish wonders with its explosive energy, it is not to be relied upon for the accomplishment of great ends, unless specially trained, unless in wedded harmony with its other half, the feminine.

This perfect duality of force is seen in the male and female parents. The male acts arid gives. The female receives and silently and secretly carries that which she receives to perfect fulfillment. She is the carrying power, bringing to pass, and while the first exhibition of energy was active, the final and crowning result could only be attained by the patient, persistent, secret work of the female.

So in the dual will the positive or masculine must act, remove obstructions, build conditions, put forth energy in the initial step of the undertaking, and then subside into the background until necessity again demands active assertion. The feminine meantime quietly holds, nurtures, and brings to fruition.

Note the man of the world, who has made a success of himself or his work. Do you find him the noisy, boasting, blustering talker? No, you find him rather the quiet, plodding, tenacious worker. He may be left far behind his more brilliant comrade. He may seem to sink even below mediocrity as compared with his associates in the social scale; yet, there comes a day when his achievements are known, when all the plodding, self-denying toil of years reaps a rich harvest. And all this, not so much the product of his brain as of his will, his feminine will.

Mark you, first he uses the explosive, powerful, masculine will to set the work into motion and then he sets to work, gradually, coolly, passively, and holds this will to the one point set into motion by the masculine will, until the end in view is accomplished.

No soul comes into this world without will, although people declare they have no will, and bewail the lack. But look deeply into their fundamental nature and character. Have you found one who has not will, and who does not exercise it in the direction of his wants? There is not one such, no matter what he may be. It may be that only with his lips he wants this or that. It may be because a friend has suggested something that he wants it. It may be he dislikes to be different from his neighbors. For all these reasons he will often fail in attaining, but if in his soul he wants a thing, so that his very being demands it, then, though all the world stands between him and his desire, he will have it.

The surface of the water will make but a light wave that recedes quickly, causing no damage, but beware when the whole body of water returns in the same direction at the same time. This is an illustration of the dual force and action of will, the upper and lower, the outer and inner, which acting in concert are absolutely invincible. This is true White Magic.

The first step in cultivating and using the magnificent power of the will is to concentrate upon a single thing desired, and then with single eye, and unswerving purpose work to attain it.

If you have found your aim, shall you not now learn how to focus your will upon its attainment? Heed then the instructions we give you and follow them faithfully. Concentration of will upon a noble purpose is the holy privilege of every soul. Your purpose is noble, you seek to live the true, the spiritual life, meaning by this, the life that accords with your highest conception of what is God-like. You have learned that the first step is to transmute self, and enthrone God; that is, your appropriation of God, which is your higher self.

CHRISTISIS

Are you willing to say: "Whatever it costs I will to attain," and to follow that? If so, then quickly will the positive force of your will sweep all obstacles aside, and make conditions by which the gentle feminine may bring to pass the thing you desire. But to the great work. You have no doubt found that the subjection and dethronement of the senses, and hence of the lower self, is not accomplished by a mere wish.

So deeply ingrained in the very fiber of your being are the erroneous views, ideas and principles inculcated by ages of perverted sense use on the part of your forefathers, as well as your own years of crude ignorance, that many a time, even after you have intellectually and earnestly accepted higher truth, your old habits and inclinations will force a battle wherein yen will be victor or vanquished. You may be tempted to judge some one, or to yield to a sensual desire. This is your opportunity to prove the value of the concentrated will.

Will you or will you not be true to your highest in this emergency? "True as life," says the soul. The heart seconds it and the will, the positive will, gathering all the forces of soul, heart and mind, hurls them full upon the temptations and they are no longer temptations. Strengthened and encouraged by victory, both phases of will gain in power and accumulative force until final victory is won. In the meantime, between these crises in one's experience there is a steady growth in power, a steadily increasing capacity for adjustment to the new standard, provided all means are taken to feed the will, and keep bright the fire of true purpose.

No inner or higher development can take place without first understanding what part the will plays in that development.

After you understand this part, you are then ready to proceed in the great work and you will begin to develop the God within yourself which we call the Christisis. Christisis is a wedding of Science and Religion, the East and the West, the love

CHRISTISIS

nature in man and the master nature. Heretofore man developed only the possibility of being master; not master of his soul and higher nature; but simply master of the brute. Now he is to be taught how to be master of self, to know his soul, to develop the love nature which is feminine, and to make his religion a science instead of a mere belief.

The more you realize the will's mightiness, the more you desire to be one with it, to let it use you as its channel. To repeat these words understandingly and reverently puts the will in the right attitude toward the divine. Selfishness shrinks to nothingness in the majesty of omnipotence.

To be filled with the consciousness of the highest, is to forget and forego the lowest. In the second step wherein you are to look at the ideal picture, have you not already found the effect to be like the loving faith of a true friend, who believes in your best only? Is not your heart warmed and your mind fired with an increased desire to be all that you admire in that fair ideal? Will you not press on with unflagging zeal to the perfect unfoldment of the mighty soul spark that God has placed within you, that part of yourself which it is your privilege to bring forth in might and glory. This is your individuality. All men have a personality, for that is born with them, but few men have an individuality, for that is the part of themselves which they must bring forth- develop- that which we call Christisis, the God within the temple.

You will now understand that the method of transmutation of the old into the new, is the explosive power of new interests and new affections. Love the right and the wrong will die of starvation and be used as food for the development of the new. Love the ideal, for then you gradually develop up to the ideal. Think only of this ideal, hold it up before yourself as a pattern. Follow it as much as you can, admire it, for to admire is to want it. And gradually, just as the rose unfolds its beautiful petals, so will you absorb the ideal, and become a part of it, transmuting the base into the good

CHRISTISIS

and true, changing weakness into power and thereby yon will be able to accomplish the things which seemed to be impossible before.

The third step, and that which will be taught you in future lessons, is the alliance of the human with the divine will. Herein lies the secret of all power and all possibilities. You must therefore face this great question and ask yourself whether you desire to continue in the same old rut, live as men now live and have lived, in misery, want and darkness or whether you are ready to live a better and higher life, suffering when suffering is necessary, knowing that it will not weaken but strengthen you and gradually developing into an individuality, knowing the good from the evil, choosing the good not only because it gives you power but because you know that it is your birthright, and gradually developing the divine within yourself which we call the Christisis.

Hold this ideal night and day, and build up some ideal picture of what you want to do or what you want to be. Hold your thoughts to the one purpose, draw a picture in your mind of something that represents this desire. If a picture of it is impossible, then let a word represent it. As a means to this end, try and set apart some time of the day or evening and go through the following exercise as you would through any physical culture exercise to develop some part of the body. And bear in mind that you are now starting to develop the soul within you which is far greater than the body:

Sit upright in a straight backed chair, with feet squarely touching the floor and with deep, slowly indrawn breath think mentally, "I will know the soul." With the exhaling breath think, "I will develop the Christisis within me and know Him." Take several such breaths, then sit quietly, assuming that you are verily developing this potent and mighty being within yourself. Keep this up for fifteen minutes each time.

CHRISTISIS

Remember that every effort that you make to overcome conditions is so much gained in the right direction, for every time you go through this drill faithfully you do just as the carpenter does who nails a board to the house he is building, gradually he will have it finished and lo, it is beautiful to behold.

Even in the ordinary routine of daily life you will find many opportunities to prove your sincerity and to test your strength. Some person may willfully misrepresent you, may say that which in other eyes might be an injury to you. Human will would resent and oppose as well as punish such offense. To you it will be simply as a trial, for you will know that to oppose is simply to add fuel to the fire and make it burn brighter. You will, therefore, simply conclude that the one having said it is one of the ignorant masses and that you, now developing the Christisis within yourself will simply ignore it and therefore, instead of adding weakness to yourself by becoming disturbed, you will add strength by forgiving it in love and controlling your feelings. By doing this you become strong for you are transmuting- changing- base feelings into the nobler ones of love, strength and power.

If it seems hard to do this, then simply hold the thought: "As I am developing the Christisis, the soul of power within myself, I must not give way to base feelings, but accept this experience as a test of my strength."

If you will do this, then you will come into touch with that divine will which rules ail things wisely and at the same time gives all men free will to do as they wish, but punishes them justly for all wrong that they do. This will give you strength, while to give way to your feelings will bring you weakness in soul and will.

In this progress toward the higher life, and especially in the training of the will, you will find that the law of growth in this, as in all realms is, that only as the lesser is lost or changed, is the greater gained.

CHRISTISIS

In the great kingdom of nature we find that the tiny bird, featherless and helpless, breaks and destroys the only protection it has, its shell, in order to emerge into the great unknown. The bird does not know where it is going nor does it question, but the divine law, forever ruling all things, has provided it with a mother, and in the breast of that mother is planted the law of love, the law that rules all things if ice live within the law.

CHRISTISIS

LESSON SEVEN

Mind is not magnetic.

The mind and soul and body are electro-magnetic when combined, but the mind is the electrical center of soul and body, because it gives out- it makes and creates soul and body.

To be electrical is to be positive or creative.

To be magnetic is to be receptive or to receive.

The mind is electrical, because it creates and gives out its own forms, ideas, and thoughts.

It is the electrical center of the soul.

It creates the soul and gives to the soul the thoughts, works and substances on which it grows. Thus the mind is the builder, and the soul is the receiver and substance of the mind.

If we take a steel bar, start up the dynamo and run a current through the steel bar, it becomes a magnet, and is magnetic.

The mind is the dynamo, it is the electrical generator in the form of thoughts, ideas, images, etc. It charges the soul with these thoughts, images and desires and the soul becomes magnetic.

Herein is the great secret of personal magnetism, but the mind must always be creating- generating, and continually charging the soul with new force.

The soul is magnetic. It responds to and receives from the mind all the electrical currents or vibrations sent out. It evolves

CHRISTISIS

and draws to it the electrical forces in form of thoughts, ideas and desires that promote its growth and enable it to direct and use properly its powers and substances for building eternal life for itself. The body is only the reflector of the soul.

The body is charged with electricity and magnetism, making it electro-magnetic.

Every thought is substance. Thought creates and molds or destroys and tears down. Thought is also electro-magnetic. When positive or creating it is electrical. When receiving or negative it is magnetic.

Everything that exists is either positive and electrical, or negative and magnetic. The plant or vegetable is creative and forming, it also becomes receptive or draws to it necessary electrical substances to promote its growth. The germ of life in the plant is its mind and is the electrical center of its soul or body. The creative germ or life force of the plant never dies for every specie is constantly reproducing and creating. The electro-magnetic forces of the plant are one aspect of the dual forces in all nature- positive and negative. They emanate from the greater forces into vibrations or currents.

A current shoots out into the ether sphere. Substance is there to receive it- these forces generate life, and life produces all things. The receptive substance must be in harmony or in tune with the electric force that it draws. The grosser the drawing magnetic substance, the coarser will be the electrical force it attracts. The electrical substances that produce animal life cannot produce vegetable life.

The substance that produces the lower animal cannot produce or create man. Personal magnetism is the highest grade of magnetism because man, as he evolves toward divinity and develops spiritually becomes finer and lighter and the nearer he attains to divinity his mind and soul (electro-magnetic substance) becomes finer and higher, and the coarse and gross vibrations are cast out or left behind.

A pure, true mind cannot receive the electrical charge or vibration of a coarse, impure mind.

Hence an evil thought has no power over a pure, wholesome mind. Minds are receptive only to that element of vibrations that attract them. These vibrations must either be of the same key or but slightly finer or coarser.

We think only what our mind bids us think.

When we think we produce something- we create a something that lives. The soul then builds upon the thoughts produced. It is similar to sorting out good and bad apples. We receive a basket of apples. Some are good, some are bad. We take the good and lay to one side- then we throw out the bad and keep the good. We have something good and wholesome and nourishing, something that satisfies hunger, helps to eliminate certain poisons in our system and helps to build up health and strength. Such is the mind that eliminates the gross, evil thoughts and builds up a perfect soul. If we allow the apples to lay mixed up together and do not make any effort to sort them, the bad ones will corrupt the good and eventually destroy them. Such is an inert, lazy, savage mind. It will destroy its own soul. The inert, sensual mind never gives out anything but slime and filth. It is a charnel house of disease and all evil. It is both contagious and infectious. It draws to it only the minds and souls like itself, for all is in harmony with nature's laws. The most evil thought or law in existence attracts and draws to it certain thoughts and laws in harmony with it.

Whatever the mind desires it creates for itself and draws to itself all other desires of similar kind. Love is the ruling vibration

CHRISTISIS

of all creation. The savage loves his own coarse, ignorant life, and is reluctant to forsake it. The hog loves his pool of stagnant, dirty water, the ignorant love their own class, evil loves evil, hate loves hate and all thoughts in harmony with it.

Goodness loves goodness, truth and virtue and manifests and attracts all laws in harmony with it. This love is the ruling force of the universe.

Love is divine only when all the grossness, the cruelty, the hog-nature, the ignorance, the evil, the hate, jealousy, envy and malice have been cast cut and consumed by the eternal fire or divine love- the Christisis.

We respond to the things we love, mentally, spiritually and physically. If an evil thought or vibration is sent by an evil mind into our aura or circle of soul, we respond to that thought if we love the evil thoughts. Our spirit also responds, our body responds and manifests the dominating, controlling influence or thought. That evil thought lodges within the mind and creates and produces its likeness. A sensual mind produces and creates a sensual soul. This soul creates a sensual body. The features of the face, the walk, the movements and mannerisms are all indications of the senses or sensual mind. Such a body, such a face, such a manner draws and attracts the sensual mind or the mind in harmony with it. Anger hates harmony. Jealousy hates purity, and these are all antagonistic to good. The jealous, envious, hating heart cannot build up a beautiful soul.

The beautiful mind creates a beautiful soul.

Root out every evil weed, tear out the thorns, the tares and the thistles and draw to you the vibrations that never destroy. Love is the highest, the strongest vibration in the universe. It can destroy all evil by responding to that which is good. Hate cannot enter the portals of love.

CHRISTISIS

For instance, if two people love each other the force of the electrical charge and magnetic inductions from one to the other can entirely destroy any foreign or evil thought force that comes within their presence. Love can build up a wall of protection around the object loved, and no energy can encompass it. Love is not lust nor evil desire. Love is desire only when the object of desire is purity, goodness, or truth. Everything loves its own, but true love is not necessarily present in passion. Strong passion may be devoid of true love.

Man is good only in as much as he reflects goodness. He loves that which he reflects. For instance, the gourmand expresses by his abnormal weight and superfluity of flesh that he is a gourmand. The miser soon tells tales on himself by his looks, his voice, his actions. An artist or musician is easily recognized in a crowd of people- by his personality- or his looks. The musician's soul is reflected in his body. And we need not look long upon the lazy, the shiftless, the sensual to determine character. Their real portrait is ever with them. No one lives behind a veil. The soul does not veil itself. It reflects itself in the body.

The sun is the soul of the universe. The universe reflects the sun. It is the likeness or image of the sun. And, as the sun is the soul of the universe so is the soul of man the sun of his body. As the universe reflects the sun, so also does the body reflect the soul of man. No matter how beautifully formed the features or body may be, they cannot hide the soul.

The soul looks out through pure, clear, straight-forward eyes, or blears out at the world in greedy, lustful, sensual eagerness. The tendencies of the soul may be concealed for a while, but let the object that attracts it most come near and in a flash the real nature of the soul discloses itself. The attracting influence may be the grace and outlines of a beautiful form, or it may be the glitter of gold, or the sparkle of the diamond. To one who knows the secret the true character is ever unfolded and no

CHRISTISIS

mantle of pretense or hypocrisy can hide the truth. Even in the voice the soul of an individual is recognizable. And the speech is the betrayer in unguarded moments or in flashes of anger, reproof or debate.

The soul makes no effort to hide itself. The mortal only seeks to hide the soul. And though the mind may be ashamed of the soul we must not forget that mind built it. The mind is not immortal. The mind dies when the body dies.

It is the soul that lives on and retains the likeness, the image, or the form of the Creator.

Just as the dynamo that made the magnet may break and be totally destroyed, so does the mind that built the soul, die and is totally lost.

In the different stages of reincarnation the mind and body are changed; but the soul changes only as it is changed by the minds that mold it in its different incarnations.

As an illustration- a wicked soul could not be created by a pure, noble mind. The mind that creates a fiendish, evil soul is abnormal, negative, evil or perverted. It builds just what it thinks. Its soul, no matter how small, receives what the mind thinks. Thus are thoughts things. Thoughts are substances. They are real. They are forces. When the soul leaves the body at the change we call death, it dwells in the sphere of other souls in harmony with itself, just as we associate with the people whom we like and who like us. Then at the time of conception at rebirth, the soul responds to the minds or desires of the souls in harmony with it. Thus he who dies a murderer in the present life, passes to the beyond and associates with the same class there. When it reincarnates, as it must, it can only be drawn to parents who are themselves murderers either in act or in thoughts.

CHRISTISIS

The mind of parents being electrical and positive at this moment sends out an electrical flash, a spark, which is received by the soul in affinity with the thoughts or desires of the parents and in this manner the soul seeks another chance for development.

The development of the reincarnated soul depends on the people it comes into contact with while in that life. Its development also depends on whether it becomes awakened to its condition and becomes obedient to the laws of improvement.

Evil thoughts destroy. Careless, sensual, fearful thoughts are evil. Thoughts of hate, envy, malice and jealousy are evil. They produce a current of poisonous substances and are manifest in the body, as disease or idiocy or insanity. All the ills of the body are caused by the evil thoughts accumulated either in the present or in previous existences.

When the mind learns to reject the evil and to send forth good, the good destroys the evil.

Mind is not always divine. The mind of God is divine. The soul of God is divine. The body of God is divine. God is not formless. The mind of God is good, is the electrical or positive thought of good, of truth, of love, of purity. The soul of God is the accumulation of good, truth, love, purity and life.

The body of God or Good is the reflection or image of goodness, truth, love, purity, life. This is slightly symbolic, but can easily be understood if one wills to understand. All is not mind, and mind is not all.

We have the Trinity- the Father, the Son, the Holy Ghost. The positive, the receptive, the transitional. The Father (mind) creates, the Son (soul) receives, the Holy Ghost (body or transitional) manifests or reflects. If all were mind, and God were all mind, then there could be no existence. God Himself could not

CHRISTISIS

exist. There must be a receptive principle. To become Christisis we must become receptive to the creative forces or thoughts or ideas of God, that is, of good.

If there is a receptive principle there must be a transition of the receptive to the creative principles- hence the body is the transitional between soul and mind.

Mind is electrical. It is the creator, the builder, the maker. To be electrical is to send out, to give. Mind being electrical is the creator, but not the submissive or magnetic principle. If mind were all, since it is electrical, it would all go out; that is, it would scatter itself into annihilation. There could be no building up. It could not exist.

Therefore God is not all mind. He has soul and He has body. But the soul is not mind. The soul cannot be electrical. It is magnetic. The body is both. It is electro-magnetic. It is the transitional principle.

Have you a mind?

If you have mind you can think. If you think you produce, you create. If you create you can have a soul according to your liking.

If you have a soul you have a body. Your body reflects both, soul and mind. Your looks, your movements, your actions, all you do and say constitute the image and reflection of your creator, your mind and your soul.

If you are veil and strong your mind and soul are healthful and strong. Weakness of all kinds are reflectors in the same way.

Have you a soul?

CHRISTISIS

Do you know where the soul is?

Some people have no souls. Why?

The Master said to His disciples. "Fear not them which kill the body, but are not able to kill the soul; but rather fear him which is able to destroy both soul and body in hell."

Who is this who is able to destroy both the soul and body?

It is not God. for God does not destroy.

God creates and builds up, and what God creates lives forever and cannot be destroyed.

You yourself, are your own creator, and you are your own destroyer. There is no power on earth greater than yourself if you but knew it.

You can create and build up and live forever, or you can destroy both soul and body. No one can do that but yourself- your own mind. There is no power on earth able to destroy your soul if you do not will it.

You can be what you will to be.

CHRISTISIS

LESSON EIGHT

On the physical plane the senses attach men to earth conditions. On the soul plane, they interpret to him earth conditions. To be attached to things or conditions is limitation. Limitation is bondage. It is not real- it is not life. Life is universal, unlimited, and in order to have unlimited, universal life we must be in touch with that law which governs universal, unlimited life. It is possible for us to come into harmony with that law because the Father made us, like Himself, unlimited in our capacities.

The earth or physical man is a slave. The spiritual man is a blaster. On the physical plane, through his senses, he is attached to persons, places, things, conditions and these attachments bring joy or sorrow. When he develops into the spiritual being he is no longer slavishly attached to these conditions, but he is in harmony with them. He can therefore have all the joys he had before with none of the sorrows.

The physical or sense man is but a child, for his desires are based on what he sees, hears, smells, tastes or touches. He eats and drinks that he may enjoy, that he may possess.

And thus the whole round of experience on the physical plane is pursued with eagerness until the end, when no longer do the vibrations of sight, sound, smell, taste or touch enslave the senses. To him whose soul is surfeited, no longer is there glad or even fair response. Then comes dullness, indifference, death, the extreme limitation.

But when the universal's supreme light of truth and understanding shines upon the illusioned soul, the awful dullness breaks, indifference flees away, and what was earthly sight becomes far reaching vision, revealing every show of sense to be but the clothing of a thought, earth made or heaven made. The

CHRISTISIS

over-arching skies, with all their splendid pageantry of day and night, the beauteous garb of nature and nature's denizens, all the varied, wondrous details of this earth, become alive with meaning.

A new world breaks upon the enraptured vision, a world so rare and fair and beautiful that this, beauteous as it is, is but a shallow image, though it be the jeweled gateway into that other, the realm of the ideal.

As the sense of inner sight becomes illumined, quick to see and interpret the real world, wherein all things are but as symbols, made to set forth thought deep with meaning, so does the sense of hearing convey to the soul the reality back of sounds that fall upon the quickened ear, and the senses turned to seek the inner meaning are become as ministers to the soul, and no longer serve as body slaves. As it is with seeing and hearing, so with all the other senses, their function is a dignity, a blessed honor conferred by the one within- the Christisis- the one who sees and hears, feels and tastes, smells and moves, yet knows that it is not he himself, but his transformed senses, his avenues of contact with the world without, that in this higher use serve as connecting links between the earth and the universal above, the sphere of the immortal souls. He lives in the same world as before, but he interprets things differently because his senses have been transformed from earthly conditions to the higher vibrations which understand things as they are, and not as they seem to be.

This being within us, this illuminated spirit, or Christisis, free, untrammeled, ever perfect, called variously the child of God, the higher self, the soul, the matchless spirit, but with any name, and in any language the indivisible, the changeless, the absolute and only real, who in the guise of soul or spirit, or deific child, or spark of eternal fire, thus expresses or reveals infinity, and its glorious individuality in what is commonly known as the human ego. When the student becomes enlightened, illuminated, he becomes a Master, he is unconquerable, always going forth to conquer, now apparently overcome, but always to rise up and begin anew because lie knows that he has not failed until he himself admits failure.

The first arena of conflict is his body, his desires. His first conquest is over the senses, for unless he can control his senses, desiring only the things that are a benefit to him, he has not made progress.

The great question which the student must answer is, "Have you been faithful to your highest ideal, the ideal you have had a vision of in the exalted moments when the heart spoke and told you what you really desired to be?"

There is nothing truly existent outside of the soul. God as the universal soul flows into all things. God is life and life exists in all things, but life as existent force is good, indestructible, immortal and invisible. The life of man is in connection with this universal life, and he can either strengthen the cord which holds him to it or he can sever the cord and stop the supply.

The illuminated man is the reflection of the father. He bears the image of that life. In the cleansed and enlightened mind God sets a fair picture of the ideal self as a pattern for the new-found life. This new life finds rich and full expression in a Godlike character.

It is for the student to draw a picture in his mind of what he wishes to be. No matter what he may be interested in, whether his inclinations are in the direction of being a successful business man, a master builder, an artist, a musician, a philosopher, the law that governs is always the same. Keep ever before you in your mind's eye the ideal self. Note its way of dealing with all conditions incident to daily life. Picture your ideal self as displaying sweet patience in your countenance under sore provocation. See renunciation marked upon your unruffled brow

CHRISTISIS

when disappointment comes. Watch its calmness in days of dark or sunny skies. Note its repose and its serenity in failure and in success. Gradually as you continue to hold this picture before you. you will grow into this condition and you will become the master of whatever you will to be.

The building of a character or of any the condition is like the building of the house you live in. There must first be the architect who will craw the plan. Unless you can give him an idea of the house you wish to build he cannot draw the plans. The same with your character or what you desire to be or accomplish. When you know what you really desire, then your mind, as the architect, will draw the building, then you must set your workmen to work, even as the contractor sets his men to work in order to build the house. Your workmen are your thoughts and the more intense they are, the more truly concentrated upon the work, the finer will be your building and the more will it be finished just as the well trained and obedient workmen of a contractor can finish a house sooner and better than the workmen who are disobedient and untrained.

Remember that you are one with the universal builder, and creator, that you are one of his understudies, that if you are faithful you can bring out all the faculties possessed by him, though in a lesser degree. Remember that you can be as calm as he is, that you can be as true as he is, that you can be as free, as gentle, as loving.

You are living in the world of souls. The world man calls flesh, but in reality it is soul. God is all and controls all. God is the life you see about you and within you. You know you have God. for you know you have life, and you also know that no power is able to overthrow universal life, and it is therefore your duty and your privilege, to come into touch with that universal life. It is the soul that senses things in their reality. When the body is dead it cannot see, hear, taste, touch or smell. It was the life, the soul that controlled it and gave it the power of sense. In cultivating the

CHRISTISIS

higher use of the senses, first you must rectify your thought of them, remove all condemnation, or stigma that in your ignorance you may have put upon them. Remember that all things in themselves are pure.

All things have a right and holy use. If you have felt contempt or repugnance toward anything, it is because of your ignorant judgment, so the first step is always the removal of every mote from the eyes and every obstruction to the view. If you have called anything impure it is because of your false views, your own perverted vision. All is good and pure for life has given all and there is no evil in life- God.

The senses rightly used are good, else they would never have been given to man. It is only the false belief and their perversion and abuse that have brought reproach and contumely upon them. "What God has cleansed call thou not unclean," so then beware of making the mistake the world makes and calling that unclean which only man's unclean beliefs have made so.

This admonition refers not alone to your senses but to all judgments concerning men, women or conditions based upon this impure view. You will find more and more as you go on in the higher life, that charity is substituted for criticism, and love for harsh judgment.

The soul's insight or illumination is able to interpret the material sight and to understand. For beyond and behind act is motive; as you look for motive you will understand and perhaps condone it, or if you discern no motive you may perceive the simple ignorance out of which the act was born, and compassion rather than condemnation will move you to brotherly kindness.

With your own emancipation from ignorance and darkness you will understand those who are still enfolded in the darkness of ignorance and error and gradually you will become free, for you

CHRISTISIS

will pass harsh judgment upon nothing nor condemn anything, for you will know that the soul is the only judge. With and through the senses comes attachment, but it is not wise to try to kill or destroy the senses. It is well to have keen senses, but it is necessary that they shall be under perfect control. Have the senses highly developed, but have them under control: be master of the senses, not let them be master over you.

Do yon love father, mother, brother, or some friend? We all do; but see to it that this love is not based upon selfishness or upon the law of possession. Let your love be love for the soul, think of the beauty of its being, of its life that is to be eternal. Admit to yourself that each soul is an individual and must be let free. You have no right to exercise arbitrary control over the one you love. Remember that love can only truly exist when there is an understanding of equality. Love is of the soul; if it is not based upon that law then it is limited and consequently not enduring.

Follow not pleasure for pleasures' sake, nor anything that can be given or taken away, but as a wise one of old has said, "set your affection on things above", for here alone are the treasures which neither moth nor rust can corrupt, where thieves cannot break through nor steal. Bear in mind that pleasures are not forbidden you, but you are warned not to be the slave of pleasure. Enjoy all things, but when anything would draw you from your high estate, then it is time to put it away from you.

With the illuminated senses all things can be enjoyed with an infinitely greater joy, because they will be rightly understood and valued for what they represent, rather than for what they seem to be.

"Seek first the kingdom of God and all things shall be added unto you."

We do not quote scripture as an arbitrary authority. If this

CHRISTISIS

statement were given to us by any man it would be just as powerful. For it rightly teaches that if the mind is illuminated, if the soul is developed, if the Christisis is born within us, then all things may be outs, for we are the masters of our destiny.

Can the beauty of a sunrise be less beautiful because you see in it a fair symbol of the dawn of perpetual day, a symbol of the majestic law that keeps the sun, moon, and stars in their places and makes possible the succession of day and night?

Can the world he less attractive when it is known as the vast schoolroom where the soul is taught life's lessons and the unity of the real and greater soul within itself?

First let your mind be opened to truth, then let the mind build the illuminated soul, and the soul will then interpret all and you will see and hear greater wonders and beauty than mortal eyes ever beheld or mortal ears ever heard. You will then know things by intuition, as the animal knows by instinct. God, the Universal Father, gave the animal instinct and it is seldom wrong. He gave man intuition, but through wrong living, wrong thinking, and wrong acting man has lost his divine heritage. Learn to know that within yourself shines the image of God, the glorious and sublime Chiristisis.

God made you a soul, He gave you a body as a working tool. He made you perfect. You are His soul reflected, imaged, and you are in reality a perfect and sublime soul. But even that which is God-made, even the most perfect building, may be disfigured so as to be unrecognizable. Man is false to himself when he invents imperfections or an imperfect God or soul. It is wrong living and thinking that disfigures his ideas, thoughts and ideals. Soul is perfect. We are all with a soul, though we may have buried it under tons of filth and slime, and we must dig away this filth and slime, bring forth the divine spark, develop and polish it until it becomes as perfect as the Great Soul, just as the small diamond is

CHRISTISIS

as, perfect and brilliant as the large diamond.

Free your soul from the senses and their illusions. Practice thinking of the One, and your conscious union with it, and ere you are aware all your thoughts, speech and acts will accord with your new and true basis, the recognition that you as a soul live in the realm of soul.

CHRISTISIS

LESSON NINE

"I and the Father are one." "I am in the world, but not of the world." This is a proof of the fact that man may be living upon the earth plane, but that it is not necessary for him to be of that plane.

All states are but conditions of mind and soul. The good man can be on the same earth, in fact, live in the same house as the bad man. Their external conditions may be the same; but their attitude of mind and soul may be very different.

Then again, "I and the Father are one," shows the student that as is the Creator so is the creature. In other words, man, through a process which we teach him, may become like unto the Creator. He has all the virtues of the Father. He has all the power, though these are in less degree. But the virtues may be hidden and need to, be brought into expression. The power may be latent and need to be developed. Through the imagination of man God walks and talks with man.

Through the voice of the conscience the Creator will talk with man, instructing him, warning him, telling him what to do and what not to do.

The only thing that the Father demands of the son is his obedience, his honor, his love and his fellowship. If the son is willing to give this, the inheritance of the Father belongs to the son. This means all things that man may need or desire so long as it is in harmony with the divine law and all that which is not in harmony with the divine law is not lasting. It is fleeting, and of the moment and the end is sorrow.

As you grow in soul illumination you will become convinced that the laws governing all things are fixed and absolute

CHRISTISIS

and that as you live in harmony with this law you will obtain the results promised by the law, no matter what they may be.

He who has lived the life, having trained his thoughts and developed the soul, thereby finding the Christisis within, will gradually be able to prove to himself and to others the efficiency of the divine law and power. The result, in his own life, will be health and strength, success and peace, and the power to provide for every need as it actually occurs. He will have strength to bear the burden that earth conditions place upon him and to fear nothing.

Such an one, having traveled the path, will be able to speak as one having authority and be able to teach others the way.

There is no failure possible when man obeys. The laws are fixed and this explains why soul development, rational thought or divine illumination is a science; it deals with divine laws, and with divine passions; it is a religion. Thus man cannot be truly scientific unless he is truly religious.

As your own re-generation began with right thinking and therefore right building of character, you will know the law of right thinking and you will know every step of the path you have traveled. You will know that all the evil that there is, all suffering, ill-health and failure are due to wrong mental conditions, and that only in right mental conditions is the eradication of these ills possible.

You will be able to help others to the perfection of their own spiritual being, and to tell them of their higher possibilities and explain to them the unfoldment or development of the soul. Thus your life becomes a ministry to your fellow beings.

It is an established fact that all success comes through observing a set system of action. This being a fixed law, it is one's

CHRISTISIS

duty to have a regular time for this great work. Dedicate some part of the day or evening to the work and during that time follow your soul development exercises much as you would take physical culture movements. For as physical culture exercises are for the development of the body so are these soul culture practices for the development of mind and soul. When you are through this exercise, let your attention be given undividedly to the duty of life that comes next. Trust the invisible forces to continue the work of development in harmony with your heart's desire, even when your consciousness is directed in other channels.

When you enter the silence for the development of your ideal, always remember that you have a noble cause in view, namely, bringing your soul into communion with the Universal Soul in the great beyond.

Know that this can be accomplished only through the thought forces, through the mental powers; for it depends upon the mind whether you can hold the attention concentrated on certain thoughts or not.

The mind also has the power of imagination, the soul being the great receiving station. Let your thoughts therefore be upon that which you wish to accomplish and remember that this ideal can be created by the mind only through imagination, for the mind images or pictures what you would be, were you to accomplish that which you desire to accomplish. The mind must imagine what it is, how it is to be accomplished and why.

The imagination is the faculty by which ideas are conceived of ultimate truth. Truth, aspiration and hope, have their roots in the imagination.

Through this function of imagination God reaches man and walks and talks with man. It is not enough merely to image a certain thing, it is necessary to hold this image through the power

CHRISTISIS

of the mind until it photographs itself upon the soul and thus becomes a drawing center.

Imagination in man becomes alive through intense desire and prompt action. All operations of the will must necessarily act through imagination, the invisible workshop of man and God.

The realm of imagination is limitless, co-extensive wit the whole universe. All that was or is to be is at the command of the imaginative mind, and if the desire is intense enough, the imagination will photograph it upon the soul as the camera will photograph an object upon the sensitized plate and bring forth a satisfactory likeness when developed. Thus does the mind, through imagination bring forth the personified idea or desire.

The universe is full of an endless variety of material from which the imagination can create thought forms. Therefore our storehouse must be full of knowledge gained from close observation in order to equip the mind with material for its best ideation.

It is not only possible for mind to construct and create in thought form as well as restore but it is a positive fact that mind does construct, create and restore. This faculty may be called reproductive, constructive and creative imagination.

Constructive imagination can execute its work only through will power. It is not only necessary to imagine, but it is also necessary that the student, through the in- tense desire of what he wishes to accomplish, should print or stamp upon the soul the thing that he wishes to accomplish. This stamping of desire upon the soul is accomplished by systematic practice in thought concentration. This systematic practice is possible only through resolute will power.

Fancy must not be confused with imagination. Between

imagination and fancy there is a distinction that fully exhibits the nature of each through different manifestations of the same power. The highest exercise of the two aspects is imagination, it creates by laws more, closely connected with reason; it has strong emotional (a moving of the mind or soul) powers, as its actuating and formative cause, aiming at results of a definite character.

However, in the undeveloped man, imagination is nothing more than a fancy, because it is not based upon any law whatever and may be totally wanting in the matter of fact person who is not even emotional.

Imagination expands consciousness arid often carries one to exaltation; for in its highest office it is the vision of an inspired soul reading arguments and affirmations in all nature of that which it is impelled to manifest.

If the student will investigate another phase of the mind's activity he will find that imagination is prolific (generative, fruitful, productive); giving expression to all literature, science and art, as well as that wonderful element of beauty- equilibrium (equal balance) of will and intelligence. By this force in the creative energy of man, all things are possible by developing and intensifying the idea which first exists in the realms of thought.

Imagination is the creative energy of man. If it is put into action by thought, which is the cause of action, and the result is an image or picture, an idea is therefore conceived; then by contemplation the mind gradually begins to perceive that the idea can be used, that it is practical; desire then springs into play and by the action of the will (which is the projective power) this idea is developed into manifestation. In this way the passive conception of the idea is converted into active imagination which is capable of creating things not yet manifested.

Imagination is the power that molds mental forms, it is the

builder of all forms in the mind realm. Unless, however, imagination is controlled and directed by reason, it is liable to create negative pictures or just what fear, anger, pride or grief suggests, i.e., images of disease, accidents, evil, death, and these are photographed upon the soul in exactly the same way as the positive creative thoughts.

No mind can be free to act as a master if hampered by such pictures as these. And as thought or mental attitude is the builder or destroyer of all power, both physical and spiritual, it is vitally important to control the imagination, the image or pattern maker, and compel it to create only right images or patterns.

Thus, if the mental images are not just what you want, discard them at once, ere you build yourself an undesirable habitation.

Pessimistic thoughts will diminish power for good. Optimistic thought works directly the opposite, bringing out the good and forming better thought-habits. Imagination is for all powers like a telescope: you can use either end, but its use will determine its value.

Brilliant ideas are not necessarily more intense than dark or evil ones; both produce results, but the results will be opposite the one to the other.

That kind of idle thinking called reverie is even more difficult to control than evil thinking. The constructive imagination of the brain-worker is very different from the kind that indulges in reverie.

Brain workers seek along the lines of greatest resistance, i.e., the literary, artistic construction. The line of greatest resistance involves severest mental discipline resulting in substantial mental products. The student now has all the laws. His

CHRISTISIS

first work is to purify the thought, to think only thoughts that are constructive, for thus the mind is cleared for greater work. Gradually the imagination becomes a perfect working machine, the student can imagine clearly the things he wishes to accomplish or that which he wishes to be; he forms a picture of it in his mind and this he holds intently, day after day, until it becomes photographed upon his soul with the power of fire, and as he does this he will unconsciously start to work along the lines that will bring him in touch with that which he wishes to do or wishes to be, and then the accomplishment will be but a matter of time.

The student must, however, always remember that there can be no perfect thought power or perfect imagination if the physical body is imperfect. The physical is an instrument used by the mind and soul for the expression of life and power. As an instrument of equal value with the mind and soul for the time being, the body should be kept in good order; since every organ has its proper function, care should be taken that each one does its duty and does it well and punctually.

Clean, wholesome conditions as to environments must be provided; simple but nutritious food is necessary. In following the higher life, it is of greatest benefit to do all things at regular times, and with absolute faithfulness. This is important in your habits of life, in your work as well as in your development exercises, for only in system can there be perfect growth.

The body, as well as the mind is subject to habits; and any habit can be easily established through forced obedience to certain laws even for a short time. There is a simple exercise which the student may take every morning or evening, one that requires but a little time and will help him to health and illumination of body, mind and soul. A cool or cold bath is of great benefit when taken either morning or evening, but is best in the morning. After taking such a bath and when the skin has been dried by friction, open the window in your room, stand erect facing the East, and while

CHRISTISIS

taking a deep breath, hold the thought, "I will gradually develop the Christisis, the being of all-power." With each exhalation, hold the thought, "Peace and love to all my fellow beings." Repeat this seven times. Wait three minutes then repeat again seven times. Wait another three minutes, then repeat again seven times. If you have little time you need wait only three breaths between each repetition. Follow this drill every morning. If you do not wish to take a bath that often, follow the drill anyhow. Should you be in ill health, the same process will bring about health, but the mantram is different. In that case you should fellow such rules for your mode of living as may be prescribed by some good teacher of physical poise, and the "bath, may be taken as before. A hot bath should never be taken except for cleanliness; cold bath always for invigoration of the system or for development. The bath need not be cold, but it should be cool.

Standing as before, and while drawing in the breath, hold the thought, "I will come into conscious touch with the center of health and will draw vitality and the life principle from the air." While exhaling, hold the thought, "Health and happiness to all humanity." It is essential that the exhaling process should always be dedicated to others, because we must establish an equilibrium in all things and in order to receive the things of the soul we must give of the things of the soul.

You must become a master of thought in order that you may overcome all things, for in the thought realm lies the power of being. When you control thought you control desires, habits, action and all things that may either help or harm you. By continuous practice, even if only a few minutes at a time several times a day. you can easily overcome wrong habits of thinking, you will be able to remove all obstructions from the mind; it will become filled with constructive thoughts. All good thoughts are constructive whether in the line of music, art, politics, mechanics, or any other subject.

CHRISTISIS

When the mind is filled with constructive thoughts there is naturally no place for destructive ones, thoughts of fear, hatred, jealousy, malice, disease, and the many other varieties of thoughts that are always destructive. The student must always remember that he is the creator of his own being, that he can change his body, his mind, his soul and make each what he wants it to be. That he can change failure into success, fear into hope, irreligion into science and religion, mortality into immortality, the soul from a dead weight into the illuminated Christisis. However, it should be remembered that this change must come about gradually. The process of development demands patience and persistence.

CHRISTISIS

LESSON TEN

The new life that you desire to live, that you should live, is the life formulated and molded into the soul of being. You have taken a momentous step when you have taken up this great work- when you try to find the universal life and to find the Christisis. The Christisis, you must understand and always remember, is the Son of God- the highly developed soul, and as such has all power, whether in the material or the spiritual. Bear in mind that spiritual development does not only mean that you will be good and pure, but it also means that you will have power on the different planes of life.

The illumination of your own soul brings you into harmony with and into understanding of the Universal Soul- the Father, the Universal Intelligence, or whatever you wish to call it. And when you respond to the call of the greater soul, it means (though you may not know it) that you have come to the end of your present state of being, that you are about to enter into the real life.

This world is a place of existence, it is the plane in which bodies live, enjoy, suffer and pass on; as a condition this world is simply a great school for souls, continually divided against itself, now full of discord or peace, vice or virtue, sorrow or joy, dislike or affection. And for this reason is it a school, to examine all souls and find out what they love best.

The soul is the life of man. The body is the vehicle while the mind is the motive power. The soul is the life of all things. Everything that lives, exists and grows in soul or in spirit. That which has no soul lives in the spirit, which is only a connecting link between body and mind or between body, mind and soul. The mind dies when the body dies. The spirit goes back to the Creator because it is the universal media, but the soul of all things under

CHRISTISIS

the sun lives on unless it has destroyed itself.

This present world gives torment. It is the soul that feels, that suffers, that is wicked or good. Man is in reality soul, either good or bad. It is this which by the fine invisible cord of self-interest, binds the soul to itself and impels it to eat of the bitter husk of experience rather than the sweet fruits of truth. Yet at last, like a wayward child, the soul comes through very weariness of the husk to ask for the fruit. Sick unto death of the illusions and glamour of the material world, the soul says at last, "This so-called existence is not life. I want no more of it. Give me death or give me life that is not mockery. "

The soul comes into touch with infinity through evolution or consciousness gained by experience or development. The soul must, after reaching the finite, begin anew upon a higher plane. It must be awakened, resurrected into spiritual life, it must be illuminated through a systematic practice of thinking and living. And through this training it will become at one with its source, for all true development or illumination leads to this one thing, At-one-ment. By thinking and living the soul life, man comes into touch with the higher life.

This process of development, of building, of finding the Christisis, is to rise from death of the flesh into resurrection- it is initiation into immortal life. When you have come to the willing renunciation of this world of existence, you are then like one who has been lost and is found, or more like one who has awakened from a long, long sleep, for in reality you did not live, you simply existed.

The universal soul life is not relative, but absolute. It is that which is. It does not change, it cannot be changed, it is ever upward. It is that which nothing can change, to which nothing can be added, and from which nothing can be taken away. It is one, indivisible, perfect whole. It is the cause of all that is. A life, that

CHRISTISIS

is, an individual life, is merely one expression of the life.

Life is of the soul, not of the flesh, hence as the soul is alive, it is that which feels, knows, acts. The soul is like the sun, while the flesh is like the world, for as the sun is the soul of the world so is the soul of man the sun of his flesh.

As the sun warms the earth and gives it life, and makes possible its fruitfulness, so may the soul warm the. earth nature of the flesh, and make possible its usefulness and power.

There is but one life, one soul, the one substance of all soul, in which and of which all exist and subsist as in a sea of omnipresent being. Every soul is an individualized soul and a center of deific power.

There is but one universal soul, of which all souls are inlets, and as there is one soul, all pervading and all inclusive, nothing in existence should be separated from it.

Another phase of the Infinite One is Being- Being which includes all beings and from which all beings came forth; it is the Divine One, the Creator, the Most High and only one.

To know and to understand the process of thought, creation, activity and expression, by which the Divine One operates in the boundless realm of infinity; to know and to understand the relation of God to man and of man to God, is the goal toward which all development tends. Without this knowledge, there is the sleep known as death, the night without a morning.

From the absolute, there can be nothing but perfection, the changeless, the omnipresent- speaking from this plane. Thus, in man is "the resurrection and the life." However, every man has been given free will, and he may allow himself to fall into matter and darkness just as far as he wishes. All men can change the

CHRISTISIS

darkness within into light. They are at liberty to draw from that universal source of light which always contains enough for all. Thus, while they are individuals, they may still come into connection with this universal light which will illumine their souls and minds; they draw from the universal, but still remain individuals.

There is but one light in the physical universe, that which comes from the sun. The light of the moon and of the stars is but the showing forth of that one light. That which glows in the fire, or radiates from the flashing gem, is from the One. So there is but one soul light, but there are many channels of expression, many jewels that reflect the light. The expressions are millions in number, but the source is ever one.

It is the same with the One Soul, the Boundless. Its tangible expression is vitality- life. Its sensible or intellectual expression is thought. Its visible expression is the body.

In man the tangible, the sensible, the visible, makes what is called the relative or differentiated expression of soul. Man, therefore, is but a channel through which God reveals Himself, for something of the universal life shows in every expression of being.

In order that man may know the Infinite he must study the finite, but he cannot know the Infinite through the outer expressions nor through the body alone. He must go far deeper than that. He must purify the mind so that the thoughts may be pure. He must illuminate the mind so that it may reflect light instead of darkness, and he must develop or awaken the soul so that he can come into conscious touch with the Infinite; then he may know.

The key that unlocks the door to knowledge is love. Hate will close it tightly, so will anger, jealousy, malice and the ether dark passions. Love for all things is the only key that will fit the

CHRISTISIS

door to true knowledge and without it nothing can be accomplished. Love is not of the body, it is from the soul. Love was before man had being, it was the light that lighted the way for the soul. Love is within the soul and the more of love there is in the soul the more light there will be in it. Love is the essence of deity, the light which lighteth every man that comes into the world.

Mind, soul and body are simply the channels through which love reveals itself to mankind or to the individual.

Love is not confined to God alone, but it is man's privilege to love purely. It is a great and mighty power given to man with which he may do good and accomplish great things. Man alone can love. All things can show affection, for that is of the spirit and forms part of the life of things, but only man can truly love. It is the Infinite Intelligence that knows, thinks and acts, not the creature. It is that which was, is and always will be. God is soul, and as surely as you have a soul, have you God within you.

Think of your inmost and brightest as the epitome of God, and the outward as the expression which may be true or perverted. The pure, unsullied, selfless love is of God. The tainted, passionate, self love is of God also, but it is polluted, obstructed, it is tainted and of the flesh. It is your duty to purify the love nature within you, to develop it, illuminate it, so that it will be a true reflection of the Universal Love.

Understanding neither the finite nor the infinite, man knows nothing of his beginning, of his present nor of his future. He is groping in the dark without a light to lead him in the right. In this state he comes into contact with the different expressions of life on the sense plane. He is simply a sense being. In this state of being he can find nothing but fleeting pleasures, disappointments, sufferings and even disgust. Now and then he seems to have power to do things, he accomplishes something, but always there is a

CHRISTISIS

loss, a falling backwards and many regrets. Through the suffering and disappointment something within him stirs, it asks for that which is not all illusion that which has a firm foundation. The soul or inner man is stirring and wants to be awakened from its sleep. It cries out for the real life. It wants to be heard. Thus will man start to seek, he knows not what he seeks, but he feels that there is something that he wants, something that is real, something that he must have. He must find a meaning in the expressions of life, or they become mockeries, a curse from God instead of blessings. And, if he is taught properly, he will find that he is the Creator of his own being, that it rests with him whether he wants reality or illusion. He begins to learn that the soul of man is the accumulated experience of man, no matter what his experience may be, good or bad.

When he awakens to this fact it is but a step to that other principle which teaches him that first of all he must think right, that he must purify the mind so that his thoughts may be good and true, in order that good and true acts may follow.

If the student longs for the true life, the real life, then he will start to think differently from what he has been in the habit of thinking. He will cleanse the mind of the thoughts that hurt and darken the soul.

He will consider his desires and search himself to find out what he really wishes to accomplish, and when he knows what his most sacred desire is, he will start to build it into accomplishment. He will formulate the desire in word or picture and around that word or picture he must build.

The greater includes the lesser, therefore the infinite soul includes the soul of man and his desires. It is, therefore, true that we live and move and have our being in God.

These facts will not help us in any way unless we put our

CHRISTISIS

knowledge into acts. It is not enough to know that there is a universal soul, and to believe that we possess a soul. We must think, live and act so as to be able not only to know that we have a soul, but to know the soul itself, to be conscious of the soul.

All this can be accomplished through living the true life. By thinking the proper thoughts we will build the proper soul, and when we have accomplished this we will know the soul, for it has become illuminated, the Christisis is found.

As the student grows in the work he will feel the change. He will find that he is becoming endowed with a new and peaceful consciousness, something he did not possess before. There will be a sense of peace, of health, of strength and of power totally unknown before.

He will come to understand that he is never alone; that in him there is a great, powerful, divine something, speaking to him, advising him, yet ever voiceless, present and felt but not always seen, ever guiding, protecting, inspiring, counseling, uplifting, empowering him, according to his need and according to his willingness to accept. The more true he becomes and the more willing to obey, the oftener will be hear the voice and feel the help of the mighty invisible force.

It is the new life that you have entered, and it will help you in all things. Whatever you desire to do, when right, you need but to formulate so that you know what you really desire and then hold it before you just as you would the picture of a friend whom you truly love. Trust in your power, have courage, let not fear nor doubt enter, and you will accomplish.

In the life it is always well to have a mantram of power. The student may formulate this himself for no general rule can be given since certain words have greater potency for one than for another. Thus, it may be that one can easily steady all his power by

CHRISTISIS

means of the words: "God is the Universal Life and Soul, and as I am a part of Him, it is within my power to accomplish that which I desire to accomplish." Another may find some other statement of truth better suited to his purpose. But each, if he is in earnest, will be guided by the Light within to formulate a statement adapted to his every need.

When you are weak, or timid, when eaten up with anxiety, or in fear of something, then hold your mantram, speak it firmly, persistently, trustfully and your weakness, your fear, your anxiety will be blown away as by the winds of a passing storm. Can you be weak when infinite strength like an exhaustless fountain is springing up within you, filling your soul with the subtle elixir of life and strength and power? When you fear, speak your words of power, fall back upon the infinite, through the light of your soul, and you will accomplish.

Breathe forth the omnipotent words: "I have found the Christisis within myself, and I therefore know the fountain of all power, all health, all strength, I can be what I will to be." Call upon this great light within for all things. Breathe it forth in the accomplishment of all things and know that it will not fail you.

God is all. That is but to say that love is all, or that truth is all. God is all these; God is all, or in all that has life or existence; but it is possible for you to pervert Him and His power and then it becomes an evil force and a force for destruction. This you should not do.

God is omnipresent, therefore He is in all things. God is the Absolute, therefore He is Goodness, Harmony, Beauty, Strength, Power, Holiness, Peace. Your soul, at the command, will rise with quivering, joyful wings and make its flight upwards as does the eagle. Time and space will not be to it, for the soul that is awakened, illuminated, is limitless, timeless and spaceless.

CHRISTISIS

How majestic is this new being, the being thus baptized with the fires of illumination. It is with different eyes that you see now for vision is no longer vision of darkness but of light.

Still, this great, new wisdom will not take from you the obligation or desire to meet every condition, with exactness and justice. Far from it. You still have all your duties to perform as you had before, but you will perform them not as duties but as blessings, knowing that you are here to work, to bless and to save. Your work in the material world may be hard, you may have little time for meditation and development. Fear not. Use wisely every moment that you have to use. Care for naught that would retard you. Keep on faithfully, cheerfully, regretting nothing, but conscientiously giving everything demanded.

When you least expect it conditions will change and your opportunity will appear before you like an open doorway; or some fair promise to your faithfulness will suddenly be fulfilled, giving you that which you have desired and which is in line with your progress forward.

Thus will the old house of self pass away and in its stead will be reared the beautiful mansion which the illuminated mind has been building- the house built upon the Rock, the Christisis, which neither hell nor death can sweep away.

CHRISTISIS

A PARTING WORD

INDIVIDUAL RESPONSIBILITY

The student Trill now understand that he cannot escape from the law of cause and effect, neither upon the mental nor the physical plane.

This responsibility, known in Eastern countries as Karma, which is in reality action of the spirit, whether in the inner consciousness, or in outward acts, is the secret force which directs our journey through infinity, driving us down into the gloomy regions of evil, of matter, and of selfishness, or up toward the luminous fields of good, of spirit, of love.

The student must understand that each effect has an adequate cause, and that each cause works infinite consequences. That which we do today is the result of former acts, and by our present actions ice are building the law that will govern our lives in future time.

It is this law which rules all mankind, for it is the law of absolute justice. However, as we are the masters of our destiny we can start to work in harmony with this law, and instead of living a lawless life we may live the life that satisfies the law. The first thing to do, therefore, is to start to think right, for when we begin to do this, we will start to act right, we will start to build in the proper manner, and while we must work out the result of past acts we will no longer commit other acts which must be worked out or other acts for which the penalty must be paid.

Today we are building for future eternity by our present actions. We determine our own destinies. We are therefore accountable for all, either for salvation or condemnation; by our own individual will, we construct our own fate.

CHRISTISIS

Knowing this law, it is also much easier to forgive our enemies and those who are trying to injure us in some way, for we know that they, too, are living out past Karmic laws and that we in some way are responsible for the part they take in bringing about the fulfillment of our punishment.

We face the absolute fact of an infinite, all-comprehending power, of which nature is the pulsating body, an eternal reality shaping the shadowy appearance of time, variously named force, fate, justice, righteousness, love, mind, God. The most essential feature of this unfathomable being or principle is, that it is an almighty reality. Confronting this fact is the other fact, our spiritual personality enveloped in matter, shrouded in personal responsibility.

The thought that we must always associate with these principles is individual responsibility. The inevitable out- come of grouping these two actualities- God and personal responsibility- is the conception that the Universal Sustainer is giving to every creature the thing that is best for it, and that each soul is in some way accountable for its condition. Suffering is only necessary to bring us to a knowledge of the law, to bring us to a certain point, and it will persist until that point is reached; until we have learned the lesson. The Universal Sustainer gives to each life that which is best for it. But each life is held responsible for extracting good from these experiences.

What we have passed through alone makes it possible for us to stand where we are today. Consequently, what we do and think today will largely govern our experience of tomorrow and all future days.

Today is the day of salvation and each happy, sympathetic thought of love sent forth and each willing act of kindness here, there, bringing a ray of sunshine into some dreary life, will not only bring us nearer to the apex of the golden Trinity, but it will lift each one to whom we administer a degree higher. Thus we will prove that we are channels through which the Infinite speaks, and that He can, through us, administer to his little ones.

Through our individuality something is bound to come forth for the resistless power of Almighty Good is behind it. This is our fate. This fact that something is bound to result from our acts is our destiny. Our freedom lies in choosing whether we be progressive or retrogressive. It is therefore a matter of real economy to learn the true course of events as soon as we possibly can, since the law of action and reaction is eternal.

To seek after wisdom and illumination is our highest privilege. The key that unlocks the store-house of future heaven-bought treasures is love and right thought. A life in which love is the end aimed at, is the key to true development, it is the key to knowledge and to all future being for through the love nature and consequent right thinking all things are possible.

Every time we hate we break the law of love. We are not love, we are hate, and our companions of thought are hate, envy, malice, and jealousy. Thus we receive as we do to others.

In the great work we must transmute or change these undesirable thoughts into these that are finer and higher. We must come to recognize that mankind, almost universally, does not do what it wants to do but rather what it is forced to do on account of having created the conditions in times past. If you could teach men the laws of thought and of justice they also would start to build differently, but it is not an easy matter to reach them.

Salvation begins with self. You know the law and therefore it is your duty to obey it. There is no excuse for you, a student of truth, to do to others as they are doing to you. If you return hate for hate you are not better than the other, you are even on a lower grade because you know better while the other may

CHRISTISIS

not. If you persecute those who persecute you, you are not on a par with them, you are below their grade, because you know the law, but in spite of it do that which is contrary to the law.

The successful life, the life that is building not only immortality, but success in earthly things as well, is that which considers only the question, "Is it right for me to do so and so?" The question usually asked of self, "Would another do thus and so?" is pure selfishness and brings about evil conditions and failures instead of success. There can be but one rule, is it right? No matter if all humanity would do differently, that does not give you any privilege to go contrary to your sense of right.

We are what we think. Each of our thoughts is held by the soul and becomes a part of the soul. From these thoughts spring action, good actions or bad actions, as the case may be.

We cannot build success, we cannot become immortal and a part of the infinite unless we think the thoughts of the infinite. In order to be truly and lastingly successful we must hold the thoughts of success and we must plan and build according to the law of success.

The only way in which it is possible for us to destroy that which is evil and undesirable is to stop holding those thoughts or giving them place in our mind, for to give them a foothold is to give them life and to entertain one bad or failure-producing-thought is to kill one life-giving, success-producing thought.

You cannot kill the tendency to evil thinking or wrong thinking by trying to force these undesirable thoughts from your mind; that will only antagonize and intensify them. The only way to get them out of the mind is to think success-bringing, soul-building thoughts for then you use up the forces given to that which is wrong in the building of that which is right; this process is called the transmutation of thought. "Overcome evil with good."

CHRISTISIS

Remove darkness by bringing in the light.

You have been taught the laws, these laws are absolute and cannot fail. If we obey these laws failure is impossible because the laws are fixed and infinite. If they were to fail, then the infinite would fail, which is utterly impossible and unthinkable.

It is admitted that time may be required in order to show results. But you must bear in mind that m the building of a mansion upon the site where an old building stands, you must first tear down the old building and you must get all the old material away, it may even rest that you destroy it or burn it up as useless wood. After you have done then you must build your foundation and the stronger you make it the better for your building; after your foundation is finished you can start with your building, constructing it step by step until you have it finished. All things require both time and patience and it is the same with the mansion of the soul, the mighty Christisis.

Be sure to search yourself, body, mind and soul and find out what you truly desire, when you know the heart's desire, then imagine the result to be accomplished and w you have accomplished this formulate your plans thoroughly.

When this is done, then search yourself, note your weaknesses, your many different desires, and take these one by one and transmute them into the qualities of goodness and strength; thus you build them into the new being.

THE END